THE BAPTIST CONFESSION OF FAITH

THE BAPTIST CONFESSION OF FAITH

A Confession of Faith put forth by the elders and brethren of many congregations of Christians—baptized upon profession of their faith—in London and the country.

𝜋𝜌 PARRĒSIA

The Baptist Confession of Faith
© 2021 by Parrēsia Ltd.

ISBN 978 1 8382829 0 5

※

This book was edited and designed by Daniel Funke, with assistance from John-William Noble. Additional editorial assistance was provided by Darrin Gilchrist.

Typeset in Adobe Garamond Pro
and Adobe Garamond Premier Pro

Printed in Glasgow by Bell & Bain Ltd.
Cover art: © Cute Designs / Adobe Stock

parresiabooks.org

CONTENTS

Letter to the Reader — ix

1. Of the Holy Scriptures — 1
2. Of God and of the Holy Trinity — 11
3. Of God's Decree — 19
4. Of Creation — 27
5. Of Divine Providence — 31
6. Of the Fall of Man, of Sin, and of the Punishment Thereof — 39
7. Of God's Covenant — 43
8. Of Christ the Mediator — 47
9. Of Free Will — 59
10. Of Effectual Calling — 63
11. Of Justification — 69
12. Of Adoption — 75
13. Of Sanctification — 77
14. Of Saving Faith — 81
15. Of Repentance unto Life and Salvation — 85
16. Of Good Works — 89
17. Of Perseverance of the Saints — 97

CONTENTS

18	Of the Assurance of Grace and Salvation	101
19	Of the Law of God	107
20	Of the Gospel, and of the Extent of the Grace Thereof	113
21	Of Christian Liberty and Liberty of Conscience	117
22	Of Religious Worship, and the Sabbath Day	123
23	Of Lawful Oaths and Vows	131
24	Of the Civil Magistrate	135
25	Of Marriage	139
26	Of the Church	143
27	Of the Communion of Saints	155
28	Of Baptism and the Lord's Supper	159
29	Of Baptism	161
30	Of the Lord's Supper	165
31	Of the State of Man after Death and of the Resurrection of the Dead	171
32	Of the Last Judgement	175
	An Appendix	179

A CONFESSION OF FAITH

Put forth by the elders and brethren
of many congregations of Christians (baptized upon
profession of their faith) in London and the country.

For with the heart man believeth unto righteousness; and with the mouth confession is made unto salvation.—Romans 10:10.

Search the scriptures.—John 5:39.

London, 1677

Editor's Note

When this *Confession of Faith* was first published, it contained the prayer that 'the God of all grace will pour out those measures of his Holy Spirit upon us, that the profession of truth may be accompanied with the sound belief, and diligent practise of it by us; that his name may in all things be glorified, through Jesus Christ our Lord, Amen.' This is our prayer over three centuries later in publishing this new edition.

Our aim has been to be faithful to the original text of the Confession, and only to make minor changes where they were deemed necessary for clarification. The Scripture proofs quoted are from the Authorized Version, with the exception of a quotation of Acts 14:23 in chapter 26, where the Confession points to the original, and where we supply the text of the Geneva Bible and Stephen's Textus Receptus. The Scripture proofs are not meant to discourage an open Bible while reading and studying this book. Scripture proofs marked with an asterisk (*) indicate corrections to the original. These corrections range from minor alterations of how Scripture proofs are presented to corrections of obvious mistakes.

—THE EDITOR

TO THE JUDICIOUS AND IMPARTIAL READER

Courteous Reader,

IT IS NOW MANY years since divers of us (with other sober Christians then living and walking in the way of the Lord that we profess) did conceive our selves to be under a necessity of publishing a *Confession of our Faith,* for the information, and satisfaction of those, that did not throughly understand what our principles were, or had entertained prejudices against our profession, by reason of the strange representation of them, by some men of note, who had taken very wrong measures, and accordingly led others into misapprehensions, of us, and them: and this was first put forth about the year 1643, in the name of seven congregations then gathered in *London;* since which time, diverse impressions thereof have been dispersed abroad, and our end proposed, in good measure answered, inasmuch as many (and some of those men eminent, both for piety and learning) were thereby satisfied, that we were no way guilty of those heterodoxies and fundamental errors, which had too frequently been charged upon us without ground, or occasion given on our part. And forasmuch, as that *Confession* is not now commonly to be had; and also that many others have since embraced the same truth which is owned therein; it was judged necessary by us to join together in giving a testimony to the world;

of our firm adhering to those wholesome principles, by the publication of this which is now in your hand.

And forasmuch as our method, and manner of expressing our sentiments, in this, doth vary from the former (although the substance of the matter is the same) we shall freely impart to you the reason and occasion thereof. One thing that greatly prevailed with us to undertake this work, was (not only to give a full account of our selves, to those Christians that differ from us about the subject of baptism, but also) the profit that might from thence arise, unto those that have any account of our labours, in their instruction, and establishment in the great truths of the gospel; in the clear understanding, and steady belief of which, our comfortable walking with God, and fruitfulness before him, in all our ways, is most nearly concerned; and therefore we did conclude it necessary to express our selves the more fully, and distinctly; and also to fix on such a method as might be most comprehensive of those things which we designed to explain our sense, and belief of; and finding no defect, in this regard, in that fixed on by the assembly, and after them by those of the Congregational way, we did readily conclude it best to retain the same *order* in our present confession: and also, when we observed that those last mentioned, did in their confession (for reasons which seemed of weight both to themselves and others) choose not only to express their mind in words concurrent with the former in sense, concerning all those articles wherein they were agreed, but also for the most part without any variation of the terms we did in like manner conclude it best to follow their example in making use of the very same words with them both, in these articles (which are very many) wherein our faith and doctrine is the same with theirs, and this we did, the more abundantly, to manifest our consent with both, in all the fundamental articles of the Christian religion; as also with many others, whose orthodox confessions have been published to the world; on the behalf of the Protestants in divers nations and cities:

and also to convince all, that we have no itch to clog religion with new words, but do readily acquiesce in that form of sound words, which hath been, in consent with the holy Scriptures, used by others before us; hereby declaring before God, angels, and men, our hearty agreement with them, in that wholesome Protestant doctrine, which with so clear evidence of Scriptures they have asserted: some things indeed, are in some places added, some terms omitted, and some few changed, but these alterations are of that nature, as that we need not doubt, any charge or suspicion of unsoundness in the faith, from any of our brethren upon the account of them.

In those things wherein we differ from others, we have expressed our selves with all candour and plainness that none might entertain jealousy of ought secretly lodged in our breasts, that we would not the world should be acquainted with; yet we hope we have also observed those rules of modesty, and humility, as will render our freedom in this respect inoffensive, even to those whose sentiments are different from ours.

We have also taken care to affix texts of Scripture, in the margin for the confirmation of each article in our confession; in which work we have studiously endeavoured to select such as are most clear and pertinent, for the proof of what is asserted by us: and our earnest desire is, that all into whose hands this may come, would follow that (never enough commended) example of the noble *Bereans,* who searched the Scriptures daily, that they might find out whether the things preached to them were so or not.

There is one thing more which we sincerely profess, and earnestly desire credence in, *viz.* that contention is most remote from our design in all that we have done in this matter: and we hope the liberty of an ingenuous unfolding our principles, and opening our hearts unto our brethren, with the Scripture grounds on which our faith and practise leans, will by none of them be either denied to us, or taken ill from us. Our whole design is accomplished, if we may obtain that justice, as to be measured in our principles, and practise, and the judgement of both by others, according to what we have now published; which the Lord (whose eyes are as a flame of fire) knoweth to be the doctrine, which with our hearts we must firmly believe, and sincerely endeavour to conform our lives to. And oh that other contentions being laid asleep, the only care and contention of all upon whom the name of our blessed Redeemer is called, might for the future be, to walk humbly with their God, and in the exercise of all love and meekness towards each other, to perfect holiness in the fear of the Lord, each one endeavouring to have his conversation such as becometh the gospel; and also suitable to his place and capacity vigorously to promote in others the practice of true religion and undefiled in the sight of God and our Father. And that in this backsliding day, we might not spend our breath in fruitless complaints of the evils of others; but may every one begin at home, to reform in the first place our own hearts, and ways; and then to quicken all that we may have influence upon, to the same work; that if the will of God were so, none might deceive themselves, by resting in, and trusting to, a form of godliness, without the power of it, and inward experience of the efficacy of those truths that are professed by them.

And verily there is one spring and cause of the decay of religion in our day, which we cannot but touch upon, and earnestly urge a redress of; and that is the neglect of the worship of God in families, by those to whom the charge and conduct of them is committed. May not the gross ignorance, and instability of many; with the profaneness of others, be justly charged upon their parents and masters, who have not trained them up in the way wherein they ought to walk when they were young? But have neglected those frequent and solemn commands which the Lord hath laid upon them so to catechize, and instruct them, that their tender years might be seasoned with the knowledge of the truth of God as revealed in the Scriptures; and also by their own omission of prayer, and other duties of religion in their families, together with the ill example of their loose conversation, have inured them first to a neglect, and then contempt of all piety and religion? We know this will not excuse the blindness, or wickedness of any; but certainly it will fall heavy upon those that have thus been the occasion thereof; they indeed die in their sins; but will not their blood be required of those under whose care they were, who yet permitted them to go on without *warning,* yea led them into the paths of destruction? And will not the diligence of Christians with respect to the discharge of these duties, in ages past, rise up in judgement against, and condemn many of those who would be esteemed such now?

We shall conclude with our earnest prayer, that the God of all grace will pour out those measures of his Holy Spirit upon us, that the profession of truth may be accompanied with the sound belief, and diligent practise of it by us; that his name may in all things be glorified, through Jesus Christ our Lord, *Amen.*

I

OF THE HOLY SCRIPTURES

THE HOLY SCRIPTURE is the only sufficient, certain, and infallible rule of all saving knowledge, faith and obedience;[1] although the light of nature, and the works of creation and providence do so far manifest the goodness, wisdom and power of God, as to leave men unexcusable; yet are they not sufficient to give that knowledge of God and his will, which is necessary unto salvation.[2] Therefore it pleased the Lord at sundry times, and in divers manners, to reveal himself, and to declare that his will unto his Church;[3] and afterward for the better preserving, and propagating of the truth, and for the more sure establishment, and comfort of the Church against the corruption of the flesh, and the malice of Satan, and of the world, to commit the same wholly unto writing; which maketh the holy Scriptures to be most necessary, those former ways of God's revealing his will unto his people being now ceased.[4]

[1] **2 Tim. 3:15** And that from a child thou hast known the holy scriptures, which are able to make thee wise unto salvation through faith which is in Christ Jesus. **16** All scripture is given

by inspiration of God, and is profitable for doctrine, for reproof, for correction, for instruction in righteousness: 17 That the man of God may be perfect, throughly furnished unto all good works. **Isa. 8:20** To the law and to the testimony: if they speak not according to this word, it is because there is no light in them. **Luke 16:29** Abraham saith unto him, They have Moses and the prophets; let them hear them. 31 And he said unto him, If they hear not Moses and the prophets, neither will they be persuaded, though one rose from the dead. **Eph. 2:20** And are built upon the foundation of the apostles and prophets, Jesus Christ himself being the chief corner stone.

[2] **Rom. 1:19** Because that which may be known of God is manifest in them; for God hath shewed it unto them. 20 For the invisible things of him from the creation of the world are clearly seen, being understood by the things that are made, even his eternal power and Godhead; so that they are without excuse: 21 Because that, when they knew God, they glorified him not as God, neither were thankful; but became vain in their imaginations, and their foolish heart was darkened. **Rom. 2:14** For when the Gentiles, which have not the law, do by nature the things contained in the law, these, having not the law, are a law unto themselves: 15 Which shew the work of the law written in their hearts, their conscience also bearing witness, and their thoughts the mean while accusing or else excusing one another. **Ps. 19:1** The heavens declare the glory of God; and the firmament sheweth his handywork. 2 Day unto day uttereth speech, and night unto night sheweth knowledge. 3 There is no speech nor language, where their voice is not heard.

[3] **Heb. 1:1** God, who at sundry times and in divers manners spake in time past unto the fathers by the prophets.

[4] **Prov. 22:19** That thy trust may be in the Lord, I have made known to thee this day, even to thee. 20 Have not I written to

I. OF THE HOLY SCRIPTURES

thee excellent things in counsels and knowledge, 21 That I might make thee know the certainty of the words of truth; that thou mightest answer the words of truth to them that send unto thee? **Rom. 15:4** For whatsoever things were written aforetime were written for our learning, that we through patience and comfort of the scriptures might have hope. **2 Pet. 1:19** We have also a more sure word of prophecy; whereunto ye do well that ye take heed, as unto a light that shineth in a dark place, until the day dawn, and the day star arise in your hearts: 20 Knowing this first, that no prophecy of the scripture is of any private interpretation.

2. Under the name of holy Scripture or the word of God written; are now contained all the books of the Old and New Testament which are these,

Of the Old Testament

Genesis, Exodus, Leviticus, Numbers, Deuteronomy, Joshua, Judges, Ruth, 1 Samuel, 2 Samuel, 1 Kings, 2 Kings, 1 Chronicles, 2 Chronicles, Ezra, Nehemiah, Esther, Job, Psalms, Proverbs, Ecclesiastes, The Song of Songs, Isaiah, Jeremiah, Lamentations, Ezekiel, Daniel, Hosea, Joel, Amos, Obadiah, Jonah, Micah, Nahum, Habakkuk, Zephaniah, Haggai, Zechariah, Malachi.

Of the New Testament

Matthew, Mark, Luke, John, The Acts of the Apostles, Paul's Epistle to the Romans, 1 Corinthians, 2 Corinthians, Galatians,

Ephesians, Philippians, Colossians, 1 Thessalonians, 2 Thessalonians, 1 Timothy, 2 Timothy, to Titus, to Philemon, the Epistle to the Hebrews, the Epistle of James, The first and second Epistles of Peter, The first, second and third Epistles of John, the Epistle of Jude, the Revelation. All which are given by the inspiration of God, to be the rule of faith and life.[1]

[1] **2 Tim. 3:16** All scripture is given by inspiration of God, and is profitable for doctrine, for reproof, for correction, for instruction in righteousness.

3. The books commonly called Apocrypha, not being of divine inspiration, are no part of the canon (or rule) of the Scripture, and therefore are of no authority to the Church of God, nor to be any otherwise approved or made use of, than other human writings.[1]

[1] **Luke 24:27** And beginning at Moses and all the prophets, he expounded unto them in all the scriptures the things concerning himself. **44** And he said unto them, These are the words which I spake unto you, while I was yet with you, that all things must be fulfilled, which were written in the law of Moses, and in the prophets, and in the psalms, concerning me. **Rom. 3:2** Much every way: chiefly, because that unto them were committed the oracles of God.

4. The authority of the holy Scripture for which it ought to be believed dependeth not upon the testimony of any man, or church; but wholly upon God (who is truth itself) the Author thereof; therefore it is to be received, because it is the word of God.[1]

I. OF THE HOLY SCRIPTURES

[1] **2 Pet. 1:19** We have also a more sure word of prophecy; whereunto ye do well that ye take heed, as unto a light that shineth in a dark place, until the day dawn, and the day star arise in your hearts: 20 Knowing this first, that no prophecy of the scripture is of any private interpretation. 21 For the prophecy came not in old time by the will of man: but holy men of God spake as they were moved by the Holy Ghost. **2 Tim. 3:16** All scripture is given by inspiration of God, and is profitable for doctrine, for reproof, for correction, for instruction in righteousness. **2 Thess. 2:13** But we are bound to give thanks alway to God for you, brethren beloved of the Lord, because God hath from the beginning chosen you to salvation through sanctification of the Spirit and belief of the truth. **1 John 5:9** If we receive the witness of men, the witness of God is greater: for this is the witness of God which he hath testified of his Son.

5. We may be moved and induced by the testimony of the Church of God, to an high and reverent esteem of the holy Scriptures; and the heavenliness of the matter, the efficacy of the doctrine, and the majesty of the style, the consent of all the parts, the scope of the whole (which is to give all glory to God), the full discovery it makes of the only way of man's salvation, and many other incomparable excellencies, and entire perfections thereof, are arguments whereby it doth abundantly evidence itself to be the word of God; yet notwithstanding, our full persuasion, and assurance of the infallible truth, and divine authority thereof, is from the inward work of the Holy Spirit, bearing witness by and with the word in our hearts.[1]

[1] **John 16:13** Howbeit when he, the Spirit of truth, is come, he will guide you into all truth: for he shall not speak of himself; but

whatsoever he shall hear, that shall he speak: and he will shew you things to come. **14** He shall glorify me: for he shall receive of mine, and shall shew it unto you. **1 Cor. 2:10** But God hath revealed them unto us by his Spirit: for the Spirit searcheth all things, yea, the deep things of God. **11** For what man knoweth the things of a man, save the spirit of man which is in him? even so the things of God knoweth no man, but the Spirit of God. **12** Now we have received, not the spirit of the world, but the spirit which is of God; that we might know the things that are freely given to us of God. **1 John 2:20** But ye have an unction from the Holy One, and ye know all things. **27** But the anointing which ye have received of him abideth in you, and ye need not that any man teach you: but as the same anointing teacheth you of all things, and is truth, and is no lie, and even as it hath taught you, ye shall abide in him.

6. The whole counsel of God concerning all things necessary for his own glory, man's salvation, faith and life, is either expressly set down or necessarily contained in the *holy Scripture;* unto which nothing at any time is to be added, whether by new revelation of the *Spirit,* or traditions of men.[1]

Nevertheless we acknowledge the inward illumination of the Spirit of God, to be necessary for the saving understanding of such things as are revealed in the word,[2] and that there are some circumstances concerning the worship of God, and government of the Church common to human actions and societies; which are to be ordered by the light of nature, and Christian prudence according to the general rules of the word, which are always to be observed.[3]

---

[1] **2 Tim. 3:15** And that from a child thou hast known the holy scriptures, which are able to make thee wise unto salvation

through faith which is in Christ Jesus. **16** All scripture is given by inspiration of God, and is profitable for doctrine, for reproof, for correction, for instruction in righteousness: **17** That the man of God may be perfect, throughly furnished unto all good works. **Gal. 1:8** But though we, or an angel from heaven, preach any other gospel unto you than that which we have preached unto you, let him be accursed. **9** As we said before, so say I now again, if any man preach any other gospel unto you than that ye have received, let him be accursed.

[2] **John 6:45** It is written in the prophets, And they shall be all taught of God. Every man therefore that hath heard, and hath learned of the Father, cometh unto me. **1 Cor. 2:9** But as it is written, Eye hath not seen, nor ear heard, neither have entered into the heart of man, the things which God hath prepared for them that love him. **10** But God hath revealed them unto us by his Spirit: for the Spirit searcheth all things, yea, the deep things of God. **11** For what man knoweth the things of a man, save the spirit of man which is in him? even so the things of God knoweth no man, but the Spirit of God. **12** Now we have received, not the spirit of the world, but the spirit which is of God; that we might know the things that are freely given to us of God.

[3] **1 Cor. 11:13** Judge in yourselves: is it comely that a woman pray unto God uncovered? **14** Doth not even nature itself teach you, that, if a man have long hair, it is a shame unto him? **1 Cor. 14:26** How is it then, brethren? when ye come together, every one of you hath a psalm, hath a doctrine, hath a tongue, hath a revelation, hath an interpretation. Let all things be done unto edifying. **40** Let all things be done decently and in order.

7. All things in Scripture are not alike plain in themselves, nor alike clear unto all;[1] yet those things which are necessary

to be known, believed, and observed for salvation, are so clearly propounded, and opened in some place of Scripture or other, that not only the learned, but the unlearned, in a due use of ordinary means, may attain to a sufficient understanding of them.[2]

[1] **2 Pet. 3:16** As also in all his epistles, speaking in them of these things; in which are some things hard to be understood, which they that are unlearned and unstable wrest, as they do also the other scriptures, unto their own destruction.

[2] **Ps. 19:7** The law of the LORD is perfect, converting the soul: the testimony of the LORD is sure, making wise the simple. **Ps. 119:130** The entrance of thy words giveth light; it giveth understanding unto the simple.

8. The Old Testament in *Hebrew* (which was the native language of the people of God of old),[1] and the New Testament in *Greek* (which at the time of the writing of it was most generally known to the nations), being immediately inspired by God, and by his singular care and providence kept pure in all ages, are therefore authentical; so as in all controversies of religion the Church is finally to appeal unto them.[2] But because these original tongues are not known to all the people of God, who have a right unto, and interest in the Scriptures, and are commanded in the fear of God to read[3] and search them,[4] therefore they are to be translated into the vulgar language of every nation, unto which they come,[5] that the word of God dwelling plentifully in all, they may worship him in an acceptable manner, and through patience and comfort of the Scriptures may have hope.[6]

I. OF THE HOLY SCRIPTURES

[1] **Rom. 3:2** Much every way: chiefly, because that unto them were committed the oracles of God.

[2] **Isa. 8:20** To the law and to the testimony: if they speak not according to this word, it is because there is no light in them.

[3] **Acts 15:15** And to this agree the words of the prophets; as it is written.

[4] **John 5:39** Search the scriptures; for in them ye think ye have eternal life: and they are they which testify of me.

[5] **1 Cor. 14:6** Now, brethren, if I come unto you speaking with tongues, what shall I profit you, except I shall speak to you either by revelation, or by knowledge, or by prophesying, or by doctrine? 9 So likewise ye, except ye utter by the tongue words easy to be understood, how shall it be known what is spoken? for ye shall speak into the air. 11 Therefore if I know not the meaning of the voice, I shall be unto him that speaketh a barbarian, and he that speaketh shall be a barbarian unto me. 12 Even so ye, forasmuch as ye are zealous of spiritual gifts, seek that ye may excel to the edifying of the church. 24 But if all prophesy, and there come in one that believeth not, or one unlearned, he is convinced of all, he is judged of all. 28 But if there be no interpreter, let him keep silence in the church; and let him speak to himself, and to God.

[6] **Col. 3:16** Let the word of Christ dwell in you richly in all wisdom; teaching and admonishing one another in psalms and hymns and spiritual songs, singing with grace in your hearts to the Lord.

9. The infallible rule of interpretation of Scripture is the Scripture itself:[1] and therefore when there is a question about the true and full sense of any Scripture (which is not

manifold but one) it must be searched by other places that speak more clearly.

> [1] **2 Pet. 1:20** Knowing this first, that no prophecy of the scripture is of any private interpretation. **21** For the prophecy came not in old time by the will of man: but holy men of God spake as they were moved by the Holy Ghost. **Acts 15:15** And to this agree the words of the prophets; as it is written, **16** After this I will return, and will build again the tabernacle of David, which is fallen down; and I will build again the ruins thereof, and I will set it up.

10. The supreme judge by which all controversies of religion are to be determined, and all decrees of counsels, opinions of ancient writers, doctrines of men, and private spirits, are to be examined, and in whose sentence we are to rest, can be no other but the holy Scripture delivered by the Spirit, into which Scripture so delivered, our faith is finally resolved.[1]

> [1] **Matt. 22:29** Jesus answered and said unto them, Ye do err, not knowing the scriptures, nor the power of God. **31** But as touching the resurrection of the dead, have ye not read that which was spoken unto you by God, saying. **Eph. 2:20** And are built upon the foundation of the apostles and prophets, Jesus Christ himself being the chief corner stone. **Acts 28:23** And when they had appointed him a day, there came many to him into his lodging; to whom he expounded and testified the kingdom of God, persuading them concerning Jesus, both out of the law of Moses, and out of the prophets, from morning till evening.

2

OF GOD AND OF THE HOLY TRINITY

THE LORD OUR God is but one only living, and true God;[1] whose subsistence is in and of himself,[2] infinite in being, and perfection, whose essence cannot be comprehended by any but himself;[3] a most pure spirit,[4] invisible, without body, parts, or passions, who only hath immortality, dwelling in the light, which no man can approach unto,[5] who is immutable,[6] immense,[7] eternal,[8] incomprehensible, almighty,[9] every way infinite, most holy,[10] most wise, most free, most absolute, working all things according to the counsel of his own immutable, and most righteous will,[11] for his own glory,[12] most loving, gracious, merciful, long-suffering, abundant in goodness and truth, forgiving iniquity, transgression and sin, the rewarder of them that diligently seek him,[13] and withall most just, and terrible in his judgements,[14] hating all sin,[15] and who will by no means clear the guilty.[16]

[1] 1 Cor. 8:4 As concerning therefore the eating of those things that are offered in sacrifice unto idols, we know that an idol is nothing in the world, and that there is none other God but one. **6** But to us there is but one God, the Father, of whom are all

things, and we in him; and one Lord Jesus Christ, by whom are all things, and we by him. **Deut. 6:4** Hear, O Israel: The LORD our God is one LORD.

² **Jer. 10:10** But the LORD is the true God, he is the living God, and an everlasting king: at his wrath the earth shall tremble, and the nations shall not be able to abide his indignation. **Isa. 48:12** Hearken unto me, O Jacob and Israel, my called; I am he; I am the first, I also am the last.

³ **Exod. 3:14** And God said unto Moses, I AM THAT I AM: and he said, Thus shalt thou say unto the children of Israel, I AM hath sent me unto you.

⁴ **John 4:24** God is a Spirit: and they that worship him must worship him in spirit and in truth.

⁵ **1 Tim. 1:17** Now unto the King eternal, immortal, invisible, the only wise God, be honour and glory for ever and ever. Amen. **Deut. 4:15** Take ye therefore good heed unto yourselves; for ye saw no manner of similitude on the day that the LORD spake unto you in Horeb out of the midst of the fire: **16** Lest ye corrupt yourselves, and make you a graven image, the similitude of any figure, the likeness of male or female.

⁶ **Mal. 3:6** For I am the LORD, I change not; therefore ye sons of Jacob are not consumed.

⁷ **1 Kings 8:27** But will God indeed dwell on the earth? behold, the heaven and heaven of heavens cannot contain thee; how much less this house that I have builded? **Jer. 23:23** Am I a God at hand, saith the LORD, and not a God afar off?

⁸ **Ps. 90:2** Before the mountains were brought forth, or ever thou hadst formed the earth and the world, even from everlasting to everlasting, thou art God.

⁹ **Gen. 17:1** And when Abram was ninety years old and nine, the LORD appeared to Abram, and said unto him, I am the Almighty God; walk before me, and be thou perfect.

II. OF GOD AND OF THE HOLY TRINITY

[10] **Isa. 6:3** And one cried unto another, and said, Holy, holy, holy, is the LORD of hosts: the whole earth is full of his glory.

[11] **Ps. 115:3** But our God is in the heavens: he hath done whatsoever he hath pleased. **Isa. 46:10** Declaring the end from the beginning, and from ancient times the things that are not yet done, saying, My counsel shall stand, and I will do all my pleasure.

[12] **Prov. 16:4** The LORD hath made all things for himself: yea, even the wicked for the day of evil. **Rom. 11:36** For of him, and through him, and to him, are all things: to whom be glory for ever. Amen.

[13] **Exod. 34:6** And the LORD passed by before him, and proclaimed, The LORD, The LORD God, merciful and gracious, longsuffering, and abundant in goodness and truth, 7 Keeping mercy for thousands, forgiving iniquity and transgression and sin, and that will by no means clear the guilty; visiting the iniquity of the fathers upon the children, and upon the children's children, unto the third and to the fourth generation. **Heb. 11:6** But without faith it is impossible to please him: for he that cometh to God must believe that he is, and that he is a rewarder of them that diligently seek him.

[14] **Neh. 9:32** Now therefore, our God, the great, the mighty, and the terrible God, who keepest covenant and mercy, let not all the trouble seem little before thee, that hath come upon us, on our kings, on our princes, and on our priests, and on our prophets, and on our fathers, and on all thy people, since the time of the kings of Assyria unto this day. 33 Howbeit thou art just in all that is brought upon us; for thou hast done right, but we have done wickedly.

[15] **Ps. 5:5** The foolish shall not stand in thy sight: thou hatest all workers of iniquity. 6 Thou shalt destroy them that speak leasing: the LORD will abhor the bloody and deceitful man.

[16] **Exod. 34:7** Keeping mercy for thousands, forgiving iniquity and transgression and sin, and that will by no means clear the guilty; visiting the iniquity of the fathers upon the children, and

upon the children's children, unto the third and to the fourth generation. **Nah. 1:2** God is jealous, and the Lord revengeth; the Lord revengeth, and is furious; the Lord will take vengeance on his adversaries, and he reserveth wrath for his enemies. **3** The Lord is slow to anger, and great in power, and will not at all acquit the wicked: the Lord hath his way in the whirlwind and in the storm, and the clouds are the dust of his feet.

2. God having all life,[1] glory,[2] goodness,[3] blessedness, in and of himself: is alone in, and unto himself all-sufficient, not standing in need of any creature which he hath made, nor deriving any glory from them,[4] but only manifesting his own glory in, by, unto, and upon them, he is the alone fountain of all being, of whom, through whom, and to whom are all things,[5] and he hath most sovereign dominion over all creatures, to do by them, for them, or upon them, whatsoever himself pleaseth;[6] in his sight all things are open and manifest,[7] his knowledge is infinite, infallible, and independent upon the creature, so as nothing is to him contingent, or uncertain;[8] he is most holy in all his counsels, in all his works,[9] and in all his commands; to him is due from angels and men, whatsoever worship,[10] service, or obedience as creatures they owe unto the Creator, and whatever he is further pleased to require of them.

[1] **John 5:26** For as the Father hath life in himself; so hath he given to the Son to have life in himself.

[2] **Ps. 148:13** Let them praise the name of the Lord: for his name alone is excellent; his glory is above the earth and heaven.

[3] **Ps. 119:68** Thou art good, and doest good; teach me thy statutes.

[4] **Job 22:2** Can a man be profitable unto God, as he that is wise may be profitable unto himself? **3** Is it any pleasure to the Almighty,

II. OF GOD AND OF THE HOLY TRINITY

that thou art righteous? or is it gain to him, that thou makest thy ways perfect?

[5] **Rom. 11:34** For who hath known the mind of the Lord? or who hath been his counsellor? 35 Or who hath first given to him, and it shall be recompensed unto him again? 36 For of him, and through him, and to him, are all things: to whom be glory for ever. Amen.

[6] **Dan. 4:25** That they shall drive thee from men, and thy dwelling shall be with the beasts of the field, and they shall make thee to eat grass as oxen, and they shall wet thee with the dew of heaven, and seven times shall pass over thee, till thou know that the most High ruleth in the kingdom of men, and giveth it to whomsoever he will. 34 And at the end of the days I Nebuchadnezzar lifted up mine eyes unto heaven, and mine understanding returned unto me, and I blessed the most High, and I praised and honoured him that liveth for ever, whose dominion is an everlasting dominion, and his kingdom is from generation to generation: 35 And all the inhabitants of the earth are reputed as nothing: and he doeth according to his will in the army of heaven, and among the inhabitants of the earth: and none can stay his hand, or say unto him, What doest thou?

[7] **Heb. 4:13** Neither is there any creature that is not manifest in his sight: but all things are naked and opened unto the eyes of him with whom we have to do.

[8] **Ezek. 11:5** And the Spirit of the LORD fell upon me, and said unto me, Speak; Thus saith the LORD; Thus have ye said, O house of Israel: for I know the things that come into your mind, every one of them. **Acts 15:18** Known unto God are all his works from the beginning of the world.

[9] **Ps. 145:17** The LORD is righteous in all his ways, and holy in all his works.

[10] **Rev. 5:12** Saying with a loud voice, Worthy is the Lamb that was slain to receive power, and riches, and wisdom, and strength,

and honour, and glory, and blessing. 13 And every creature which is in heaven, and on the earth, and under the earth, and such as are in the sea, and all that are in them, heard I saying, Blessing, and honour, and glory, and power, be unto him that sitteth upon the throne, and unto the Lamb for ever and ever. 14 And the four beasts said, Amen. And the four and twenty elders fell down and worshipped him that liveth for ever and ever.

3. In this divine and infinite Being there are three subsistences, the Father, the Word (or Son), and Holy Spirit,[1] of one substance, power, and eternity, each having the whole divine essence, yet the essence undivided,[2] the Father is of none, neither begotten nor proceeding, the Son is eternally begotten of the Father,[3] the Holy Spirit proceeding from the Father and the Son,[4] all infinite, without beginning, therefore but one God, who is not to be divided in nature and being; but distinguished by several peculiar, relative properties, and personal relations; which doctrine of the Trinity is the foundation of all our communion with God, and comfortable dependence on him.

[1] **1 John 5:7** For there are three that bear record in heaven, the Father, the Word, and the Holy Ghost: and these three are one. **Matt. 28:19** Go ye therefore, and teach all nations, baptizing them in the name of the Father, and of the Son, and of the Holy Ghost. **2 Cor. 13:14** The grace of the Lord Jesus Christ, and the love of God, and the communion of the Holy Ghost, be with you all. Amen.

[2] **Exod. 3:14** And God said unto Moses, I AM THAT I AM: and he said, Thus shalt thou say unto the children of Israel, I AM hath sent me unto you. **John 14:11** Believe me that I am in the Father, and the Father in me: or else believe me for the very works' sake.

II. OF GOD AND OF THE HOLY TRINITY

1 **Cor. 8:6** But to us there is but one God, the Father, of whom are all things, and we in him; and one Lord Jesus Christ, by whom are all things, and we by him.

[3] **John 1:14** And the Word was made flesh, and dwelt among us, (and we beheld his glory, the glory as of the only begotten of the Father,) full of grace and truth. 18 No man hath seen God at any time, the only begotten Son, which is in the bosom of the Father, he hath declared him.

[4] **John 15:26** But when the Comforter is come, whom I will send unto you from the Father, even the Spirit of truth, which proceedeth from the Father, he shall testify of me. **Gal. 4:6** And because ye are sons, God hath sent forth the Spirit of his Son into your hearts, crying, Abba, Father.

3

OF GOD'S DECREE

GOD HATH *decreed* in himself from all eternity, by the most wise and holy counsel of his own will, freely and unchangeably, all things whatsoever comes to pass;[1] yet so as thereby is God neither the author of sin, nor hath fellowship with any therein,[2] nor is violence offered to the will of the creature, nor yet is the liberty, or contingency of second causes taken away, but rather established,[3] in which appears his wisdom in disposing all things, and power, and faithfulness in accomplishing his *decree*.[4]

[1] **Isa. 46:10** Declaring the end from the beginning, and from ancient times the things that are not yet done, saying, My counsel shall stand, and I will do all my pleasure. **Eph. 1:11** In whom also we have obtained an inheritance, being predestinated according to the purpose of him who worketh all things after the counsel of his own will. **Heb. 6:17** Wherein God, willing more abundantly to shew unto the heirs of promise the immutability of his counsel, confirmed it by an oath. **Rom. 9:15** For he saith to Moses, I will have mercy on whom I will have mercy, and I will have compassion on whom I will have compassion. **18** Therefore

hath he mercy on whom he will have mercy, and whom he will he hardeneth.

[2] **Jas. 1:15** Then when lust hath conceived, it bringeth forth sin: and sin, when it is finished, bringeth forth death. 17 Every good gift and every perfect gift is from above, and cometh down from the Father of lights, with whom is no variableness, neither shadow of turning. **1 John 1:5** This then is the message which we have heard of him, and declare unto you, that God is light, and in him is no darkness at all.

[3] **Acts 4:27** For of a truth against thy holy child Jesus, whom thou hast anointed, both Herod, and Pontius Pilate, with the Gentiles, and the people of Israel, were gathered together, 28 For to do whatsoever thy hand and thy counsel determined before to be done. **John 19:11** Jesus answered, Thou couldest have no power at all against me, except it were given thee from above: therefore he that delivered me unto thee hath the greater sin.

[4] **Num. 23:19** God is not a man, that he should lie; neither the son of man, that he should repent: hath he said, and shall he not do it? or hath he spoken, and shall he not make it good? **Eph. 1:3** Blessed be the God and Father of our Lord Jesus Christ, who hath blessed us with all spiritual blessings in heavenly places in Christ: 4 According as he hath chosen us in him before the foundation of the world, that we should be holy and without blame before him in love: 5 Having predestinated us unto the adoption of children by Jesus Christ to himself, according to the good pleasure of his will.

2. Although God knoweth whatsoever may, or can come to pass upon all supposed conditions;[1] yet hath he not *decreed* any thing, because he foresaw it as future, or as that which would come to pass upon such conditions.[2]

III. OF GOD'S DECREE

[1] **Acts 15:18** Known unto God are all his works from the beginning of the world.

[2] **Rom. 9:11** For the children being not yet born, neither having done any good or evil, that the purpose of God according to election might stand, not of works, but of him that calleth. **13** As it is written, Jacob have I loved, but Esau have I hated. **16** So then it is not of him that willeth, nor of him that runneth, but of God that sheweth mercy. **18** Therefore hath he mercy on whom he will have mercy, and whom he will he hardeneth.

3. By the *decree* of God for the manifestation of his glory some men and angels, are predestinated, or fore-ordained to eternal life,[1] through Jesus Christ to the praise of his glorious grace;[2] others being left to act in their sin to their just condemnation, to the praise of his glorious justice.[3]

[1] **1 Tim. 5:21** I charge thee before God, and the Lord Jesus Christ, and the elect angels, that thou observe these things without preferring one before another, doing nothing by partiality. **Matt. 25:41** Then shall he say also unto them on the left hand, Depart from me, ye cursed, into everlasting fire, prepared for the devil and his angels.

[2] **Eph. 1:5** Having predestinated us unto the adoption of children by Jesus Christ to himself, according to the good pleasure of his will, **6** To the praise of the glory of his grace, wherein he hath made us accepted in the beloved.

[3] **Rom. 9:22** What if God, willing to shew his wrath, and to make his power known, endured with much longsuffering the vessels of wrath fitted to destruction: **23** And that he might make known the riches of his glory on the vessels of mercy, which he had afore prepared unto glory. **Jude 4** For there are certain men crept in

unawares, who were before of old ordained to this condemnation, ungodly men, turning the grace of our God into lasciviousness, and denying the only Lord God, and our Lord Jesus Christ.

4. These angels and men thus predestinated, and foreordained, are particularly, and unchangeably designed; and their number so certain, and definite, that it cannot be either increased, or diminished.[1]

[1] **2 Tim. 2:19** Nevertheless the foundation of God standeth sure, having this seal, The Lord knoweth them that are his. And, Let every one that nameth the name of Christ depart from iniquity. **John 13:18** I speak not of you all: I know whom I have chosen: but that the scripture may be fulfilled, He that eateth bread with me hath lifted up his heel against me.

5. Those of mankind that are predestinated to life, God before the foundation of the world was laid, according to his eternal and immutable purpose, and the secret counsel and good pleasure of his will, hath chosen in Christ unto everlasting glory, out of his mere free grace and love;[1] without any other thing in the creature as a condition or cause moving him thereunto.[2]

[1] **Eph. 1:4** According as he hath chosen us in him before the foundation of the world, that we should be holy and without blame before him in love. **9** Having made known unto us the mystery of his will, according to his good pleasure which he hath purposed in himself. **11** In whom also we have obtained an inheritance, being predestinated according to the purpose of

him who worketh all things after the counsel of his own will. **Rom. 8:30** Moreover whom he did predestinate, them he also called: and whom he called, them he also justified: and whom he justified, them he also glorified. **2 Tim. 1:9** Who hath saved us, and called us with an holy calling, not according to our works, but according to his own purpose and grace, which was given us in Christ Jesus before the world began. **1 Thess. 5:9** For God hath not appointed us to wrath, but to obtain salvation by our Lord Jesus Christ.

[2] **Rom. 9:13** As it is written, Jacob have I loved, but Esau have I hated. **16** So then it is not of him that willeth, nor of him that runneth, but of God that sheweth mercy. **Eph. 1:6** To the praise of the glory of his grace, wherein he hath made us accepted in the beloved. **12** That we should be to the praise of his glory, who first trusted in Christ.

6. As God hath appointed the elect unto glory, so he hath by the eternal and most free purpose of his will, fore-ordained all the means thereunto,[1] wherefore they who are elected, being fallen in Adam, are redeemed by Christ,[2] are effectually called unto faith in Christ, by his Spirit working in due season, are justified, adopted, sanctified,[3] and kept by his power through faith unto salvation;[4] neither are any other redeemed by Christ, or effectually called, justified, adopted, sanctified,and saved, but the elect only.[5]

[1] **1 Pet. 1:2** Elect according to the foreknowledge of God the Father, through sanctification of the Spirit, unto obedience and sprinkling of the blood of Jesus Christ: Grace unto you, and peace, be multiplied. **2 Thess. 2:13** But we are bound to give thanks alway to God for you, brethren beloved of the Lord, because God hath

from the beginning chosen you to salvation through sanctification of the Spirit and belief of the truth.

[2] **1 Thess. 5:9** For God hath not appointed us to wrath, but to obtain salvation by our Lord Jesus Christ, **10** Who died for us, that, whether we wake or sleep, we should live together with him.

[3] **Rom. 8:30** Moreover whom he did predestinate, them he also called: and whom he called, them he also justified: and whom he justified, them he also glorified. **2 Thess. 2:13** But we are bound to give thanks alway to God for you, brethren beloved of the Lord, because God hath from the beginning chosen you to salvation through sanctification of the Spirit and belief of the truth.

[4] **1 Pet. 1:5** Who are kept by the power of God through faith unto salvation ready to be revealed in the last time.

[5] **John 10:26** But ye believe not, because ye are not of my sheep, as I said unto you. **John 17:9** I pray for them: I pray not for the world, but for them which thou hast given me; for they are thine. **John 6:64** But there are some of you that believe not. For Jesus knew from the beginning who they were that believed not, and who should betray him.

7. The doctrine of this high mystery of predestination is to be handled with special prudence, and care; that men attending the will of God revealed in his word, and yielding obedience thereunto, may from the certainty of their effectual vocation, be assured of their eternal election;[1] so shall this doctrine afford matter of praise, reverence, and admiration of God,[2] and of humility,[3] diligence, and abundant consolation, to all that sincerely obey the gospel.[4]

[1] **1 Thess. 1:4** Knowing, brethren beloved, your election of God. **5** For our gospel came not unto you in word only, but also in

III. OF GOD'S DECREE

power, and in the Holy Ghost, and in much assurance; as ye know what manner of men we were among you for your sake. **2 Pet. 1:10** Wherefore the rather, brethren, give diligence to make your calling and election sure: for if ye do these things, ye shall never fall.

[2] **Eph. 1:6** To the praise of the glory of his grace, wherein he hath made us accepted in the beloved. **Rom. 11:33** O the depth of the riches both of the wisdom and knowledge of God! how unsearchable are his judgments, and his ways past finding out!

[3] **Rom. 11:5** Even so then at this present time also there is a remnant according to the election of grace. 6 And if by grace, then is it no more of works: otherwise grace is no more grace. But if it be of works, then is it no more grace: otherwise work is no more work.

[4] **Luke 10:20** Notwithstanding in this rejoice not, that the spirits are subject unto you; but rather rejoice, because your names are written in heaven.

4

OF CREATION

IN THE BEGINNING it pleased *God* the Father, Son, and Holy Spirit,[1] for the manifestation of the glory of his eternal power, wisdom, and goodness,[2] to *create* or *make* the world, and all things therein, whether visible or invisible, in the space of six days, and all very good.[3]

[1] **John 1:2** The same was in the beginning with God. 3 All things were made by him; and without him was not any thing made that was made. **Heb. 1:2** Hath in these last days spoken unto us by his Son, whom he hath appointed heir of all things, by whom also he made the worlds. **Job 26:13** By his spirit he hath garnished the heavens; his hand hath formed the crooked serpent.

[2] **Rom. 1:20** For the invisible things of him from the creation of the world are clearly seen, being understood by the things that are made, even his eternal power and Godhead; so that they are without excuse.

[3] **Col. 1:16** For by him were all things created, that are in heaven, and that are in earth, visible and invisible, whether they be thrones, or dominions, or principalities, or powers: all things were created by him, and for him. **Gen. 2:1** Thus the heavens

and the earth were finished, and all the host of them. 2 And on the seventh day God ended his work which he had made; and he rested on the seventh day from all his work which he had made.

2. After God had made all other creatures, he *created* man, male and female,[1] with reasonable and immortal souls,[2] rendering them fit unto that life to God, for which they were *created;* being made after the image of God, in knowledge, righteousness, and true holiness;[3] having the law of God written in their hearts, and power to fulfil it;[4] and yet under a possibility of transgressing, being left to the liberty of their own will, which was subject to change.[5]

[1] **Gen. 1:27** So God created man in his own image, in the image of God created he him; male and female created he them.

[2] **Gen. 2:7** And the LORD God formed man of the dust of the ground, and breathed into his nostrils the breath of life; and man became a living soul.

[3] **Eccl. 7:29** Lo, this only have I found, that God hath made man upright; but they have sought out many inventions. **Gen. 1:26** And God said, Let us make man in our image, after our likeness: and let them have dominion over the fish of the sea, and over the fowl of the air, and over the cattle, and over all the earth, and over every creeping thing that creepeth upon the earth.

[4] **Rom. 2:14** For when the Gentiles, which have not the law, do by nature the things contained in the law, these, having not the law, are a law unto themselves: **15** Which shew the work of the law written in their hearts, their conscience also bearing witness, and their thoughts the mean while accusing or else excusing one another.

[5] **Gen. 3:6** And when the woman saw that the tree was good for food, and that it was pleasant to the eyes, and a tree to be desired

to make one wise, she took of the fruit thereof, and did eat, and gave also unto her husband with her; and he did eat.

3. Besides the law written in their hearts, they received a command not to eat of the tree of knowledge of good and evil;[1] which whilst they kept, they were happy in their communion with God, and had dominion over the creatures.[2]

[1] ***Gen. 2:17** But of the tree of the knowledge of good and evil, thou shalt not eat of it: for in the day that thou eatest thereof thou shalt surely die. **Gen. 3:8** And they heard the voice of the LORD God walking in the garden in the cool of the day: and Adam and his wife hid themselves from the presence of the LORD God amongst the trees of the garden. **9** And the LORD God called unto Adam, and said unto him, Where art thou? **10** And he said, I heard thy voice in the garden, and I was afraid, because I was naked; and I hid myself.

[2] **Gen. 1:26** And God said, Let us make man in our image, after our likeness: and let them have dominion over the fish of the sea, and over the fowl of the air, and over the cattle, and over all the earth, and over every creeping thing that creepeth upon the earth. **28** And God blessed them, and God said unto them, Be fruitful, and multiply, and replenish the earth, and subdue it: and have dominion over the fish of the sea, and over the fowl of the air, and over every living thing that moveth upon the earth.

5

OF DIVINE PROVIDENCE

GOD THE GOOD *Creator* of all things, in *his* infinite power, and wisdom, doth uphold, direct, dispose, and govern all creatures, and things,[1] from the greatest even to the least,[2] by *his* most wise and holy providence, to the end for the which they were *created;* according unto *his* infallible foreknowledge, and the free and immutable counsel of *his* own will; to the praise of the glory of *his* wisdom, power, justice, infinite goodness and mercy.[3]

> [1] **Heb. 1:3** Who being the brightness of his glory, and the express image of his person, and upholding all things by the word of his power, when he had by himself purged our sins, sat down on the right hand of the Majesty on high. **Job 38:11** And said, Hitherto shalt thou come, but no further: and here shall thy proud waves be stayed? **Isa. 46:10** Declaring the end from the beginning, and from ancient times the things that are not yet done, saying, My counsel shall stand, and I will do all my pleasure: **11** Calling a ravenous bird from the east, the man that executeth my counsel from a far country: yea, I have spoken it, I will also bring it to pass; I have purposed it, I will also do it. **Ps. 135:6** Whatsoever

the LORD pleased, that did he in heaven, and in earth, in the seas, and all deep places.

[2] **Matt. 10:29** Are not two sparrows sold for a farthing? and one of them shall not fall on the ground without your Father. 30 But the very hairs of your head are all numbered. 31 Fear ye not therefore, ye are of more value than many sparrows.

[3] **Eph. 1:11** In whom also we have obtained an inheritance, being predestinated according to the purpose of him who worketh all things after the counsel of his own will.

2. Although in relation to the foreknowledge and *decree* of *God,* the first cause, all things come to pass immutably and infallibly;[1] so that there is not any thing, befalls any by chance, or without *his providence;*[2] yet by the same *providence* he ordereth them to fall out, according to the nature of second causes, either necessarily, freely, or contingently.[3]

[1] **Acts 2:23** Him, being delivered by the determinate counsel and foreknowledge of God, ye have taken, and by wicked hands have crucified and slain.

[2] **Prov. 16:33** The lot is cast into the lap; but the whole disposing thereof is of the LORD.

[3] **Gen. 8:22** While the earth remaineth, seedtime and harvest, and cold and heat, and summer and winter, and day and night shall not cease.

3. God in *his* ordinary *providence* maketh use of means;[1] yet is free to work, without,[2] above,[3] and against[4] them at *his* pleasure.

V. OF DIVINE PROVIDENCE

[1] **Acts 27:31** Paul said to the centurion and to the soldiers, Except these abide in the ship, ye cannot be saved. 44 And the rest, some on boards, and some on broken pieces of the ship. And so it came to pass, that they escaped all safe to land. **Isa. 55:10** For as the rain cometh down, and the snow from heaven, and returneth not thither, but watereth the earth, and maketh it bring forth and bud, that it may give seed to the sower, and bread to the eater: 11 So shall my word be that goeth forth out of my mouth: it shall not return unto me void, but it shall accomplish that which I please, and it shall prosper in the thing whereto I sent it.

[2] **Hos. 1:7** But I will have mercy upon the house of Judah, and will save them by the LORD their God, and will not save them by bow, nor by sword, nor by battle, by horses, nor by horsemen.

[3] **Rom. 4:19** And being not weak in faith, he considered not his own body now dead, when he was about an hundred years old, neither yet the deadness of Sarah's womb: 20 He staggered not at the promise of God through unbelief; but was strong in faith, giving glory to God; 21 And being fully persuaded that, what he had promised, he was able also to perform.

[4] **Dan. 3:27** And the princes, governors, and captains, and the king's counsellors, being gathered together, saw these men, upon whose bodies the fire had no power, nor was an hair of their head singed, neither were their coats changed, nor the smell of fire had passed on them.

4. The almighty power, unsearchable wisdom, and *infinite* goodness of *God,* so far manifest themselves in *his providence,* that *his* determinate counsel extendeth itself even to the first fall, and all other sinful actions both of angels, and men;[1] (and that not by a bare permission) which also he most wisely

and powerfully boundeth, and otherwise ordereth, and governeth,[2] in a manifold dispensation to *his* most holy ends:[3] yet so, as the sinfulness of their acts proceedeth only from the creatures, and not from *God;* who being most holy and righteous, neither is nor can be, the author or approver of sin.[4]

[1] **Rom. 11:32** For God hath concluded them all in unbelief, that he might have mercy upon all. 33 O the depth of the riches both of the wisdom and knowledge of God! how unsearchable are his judgments, and his ways past finding out! 34 For who hath known the mind of the Lord? or who hath been his counsellor? **2 Sam. 24:1** And again the anger of the LORD was kindled against Israel, and he moved David against them to say, Go, number Israel and Judah. **1 Chr. 21:1** And Satan stood up against Israel, and provoked David to number Israel.

[2] **2 Kgs. 19:28** Because thy rage against me and thy tumult is come up into mine ears, therefore I will put my hook in thy nose, and my bridle in thy lips, and I will turn thee back by the way by which thou camest. **Ps. 76:10** Surely the wrath of man shall praise thee: the remainder of wrath shalt thou restrain.

[3] **Gen. 50:20** But as for you, ye thought evil against me; but God meant it unto good, to bring to pass, as it is this day, to save much people alive. **Isa. 10:6** I will send him against an hypocritical nation, and against the people of my wrath will I give him a charge, to take the spoil, and to take the prey, and to tread them down like the mire of the streets. 7 Howbeit he meaneth not so, neither doth his heart think so; but it is in his heart to destroy and cut off nations not a few. 12 Wherefore it shall come to pass, that when the Lord hath performed his whole work upon mount Zion and on Jerusalem, I will punish the fruit of the stout heart of the king of Assyria, and the glory of his high looks.

V. OF DIVINE PROVIDENCE

[4] **Ps. 50:21** These things hast thou done, and I kept silence; thou thoughtest that I was altogether such an one as thyself: but I will reprove thee, and set them in order before thine eyes. **1 John 2:16** For all that is in the world, the lust of the flesh, and the lust of the eyes, and the pride of life, is not of the Father, but is of the world.

5. The most wise, righteous, and gracious *God,* doth oftentimes, leave for a season *his* own children to manifold temptations, and the corruptions of their own heart, to chastise them for their former sins, or to discover unto them the hidden strength of corruption, and deceitfulness of their hearts, that they may be humbled;[1] and to raise them to a more close, and constant dependence for their support, upon himself; and to make them more watchful against all future occasions of sin, and for other just and holy ends.

So that whatsoever befalls any of his elect is by his appointment, for his glory, and their good.[2]

[1] **2 Chr. 32:25** But Hezekiah rendered not again according to the benefit done unto him; for his heart was lifted up: therefore there was wrath upon him, and upon Judah and Jerusalem. 26 Notwithstanding Hezekiah humbled himself for the pride of his heart, both he and the inhabitants of Jerusalem, so that the wrath of the LORD came not upon them in the days of Hezekiah. 31 Howbeit in the business of the ambassadors of the princes of Babylon, who sent unto him to enquire of the wonder that was done in the land, God left him, to try him, that he might know all that was in his heart. **2 Sam. 24:1** And again the anger of the LORD was kindled against Israel, and he moved David against them to say, Go, number Israel and Judah. **2 Cor. 12:7** And lest I should be exalted above measure through the abundance of the revelations, there

was given to me a thorn in the flesh, the messenger of Satan to buffet me, lest I should be exalted above measure. 8 For this thing I besought the Lord thrice, that it might depart from me. 9 And he said unto me, My grace is sufficient for thee: for my strength is made perfect in weakness. Most gladly therefore will I rather glory in my infirmities, that the power of Christ may rest upon me.

[2] **Rom. 8:28** And we know that all things work together for good to them that love God, to them who are the called according to his purpose.

6. As for those wicked and ungodly men, whom God as a righteous judge, for former sin doth blind and harden;[1] from them he not only withholdeth his grace, whereby they might have been enlightened in their understanding, and wrought upon in their hearts:[2] but sometimes also withdraweth the gifts which they had,[3] and exposeth them to such objects as their *corruptions* makes occasion of sin;[4] and withal gives them over to their own lusts, the temptations of the world, and the power of Satan,[5] whereby it comes to pass, that they harden themselves, even under those means which God useth for the softening of others.[6]

[1] **Rom. 1:24** Wherefore God also gave them up to uncleanness through the lusts of their own hearts, to dishonour their own bodies between themselves. 26 For this cause God gave them up unto vile affections: for even their women did change the natural use into that which is against nature. 28 And even as they did not like to retain God in their knowledge, God gave them over to a reprobate mind, to do those things which are not convenient. **Rom. 11:7** What then? Israel hath not obtained that which he seeketh for; but the election hath obtained it, and the rest were

blinded. 8 (According as it is written, God hath given them the spirit of slumber, eyes that they should not see, and ears that they should not hear;) unto this day.

² **Deut. 29:4** Yet the Lord hath not given you an heart to perceive, and eyes to see, and ears to hear, unto this day.

³ **Matt. 13:12** For whosoever hath, to him shall be given, and he shall have more abundance: but whosoever hath not, from him shall be taken away even that he hath.

⁴ **Deut. 2:30** But Sihon king of Heshbon would not let us pass by him: for the Lord thy God hardened his spirit, and made his heart obstinate, that he might deliver him into thy hand, as appeareth this day. **2 Kgs. 8:12** And Hazael said, Why weepeth my lord? And he answered, Because I know the evil that thou wilt do unto the children of Israel: their strong holds wilt thou set on fire, and their young men wilt thou slay with the sword, and wilt dash their children, and rip up their women with child. 13 And Hazael said, But what, is thy servant a dog, that he should do this great thing? And Elisha answered, The Lord hath shewed me that thou shalt be king over Syria.

⁵ **Ps. 81:11** But my people would not hearken to my voice; and Israel would none of me. 12 So I gave them up unto their own hearts' lust: and they walked in their own counsels. **2 Thess. 2:10** And with all deceivableness of unrighteousness in them that perish; because they received not the love of the truth, that they might be saved. 11 And for this cause God shall send them strong delusion, that they should believe a lie: 12 That they all might be damned who believed not the truth, but had pleasure in unrighteousness.

⁶ **Exod. 8:15** But when Pharaoh saw that there was respite, he hardened his heart, and hearkened not unto them; as the Lord had said. 32 And Pharaoh hardened his heart at this time also, neither would he let the people go. **Isa. 6:9** And he said, Go, and tell this people, Hear ye indeed, but understand not; and see ye

indeed, but perceive not. 10 Make the heart of this people fat, and make their ears heavy, and shut their eyes; lest they see with their eyes, and hear with their ears, and understand with their heart, and convert, and be healed. **1 Pet. 2:7** Unto you therefore which believe he is precious: but unto them which be disobedient, the stone which the builders disallowed, the same is made the head of the corner, **8** And a stone of stumbling, and a rock of offence, even to them which stumble at the word, being disobedient: whereunto also they were appointed.

7. As the *providence* of *God* doth in general reach to all *creatures,* so after a most special manner it taketh care of his Church, and disposeth of all things to the good thereof.[1]

[1] **1 Tim. 4:10** For therefore we both labour and suffer reproach, because we trust in the living God, who is the Saviour of all men, specially of those that believe. **Amos 9:8** Behold, the eyes of the Lord God are upon the sinful kingdom, and I will destroy it from off the face of the earth; saving that I will not utterly destroy the house of Jacob, saith the Lord. **9** For, lo, I will command, and I will sift the house of Israel among all nations, like as corn is sifted in a sieve, yet shall not the least grain fall upon the earth. **Isa. 43:3** For I am the Lord thy God, the Holy One of Israel, thy Saviour: I gave Egypt for thy ransom, Ethiopia and Seba for thee. **4** Since thou wast precious in my sight, thou hast been honourable, and I have loved thee: therefore will I give men for thee, and people for thy life. **5** Fear not: for I am with thee: I will bring thy seed from the east, and gather thee from the west.

6

OF THE FALL OF MAN, OF SIN, AND OF THE PUNISHMENT THEREOF

ALTHOUGH *God created man* upright, and perfect, and gave him a righteous law, which had been unto life had he kept it, and threatened death upon the breach thereof;[1] yet he did not long abide in this honour; Satan using the subtilty of the serpent to seduce *Eve,* then by her seducing *Adam,* who without any compulsion, did wilfully transgress the law of their *creation,* and the command given unto them, in eating the forbidden fruit;[2] which God was pleased according to *his* wise and holy *counsel* to permit, having purposed to order it, to *his* own glory.

[1] **Gen. 2:16** And the Lord God commanded the man, saying, Of every tree of the garden thou mayest freely eat: **17** But of the tree of the knowledge of good and evil, thou shalt not eat of it: for in the day that thou eatest thereof thou shalt surely die.

[2] **Gen. 3:12** And the man said, The woman whom thou gavest to be with me, she gave me of the tree, and I did eat. **13** And the Lord God said unto the woman, What is this that thou hast done? And the woman said, The serpent beguiled me, and I

did eat. **2 Cor. 11:3** But I fear, lest by any means, as the serpent beguiled Eve through his subtilty, so your minds should be corrupted from the simplicity that is in Christ.

2. Our first *parents* by this *sin,* fell from their original righteousness and communion with *God,* and we in them, whereby death came upon all;[1] all becoming dead in *sin,*[2] and wholly defiled, in all the faculties, and parts, of soul, and body.[3]

[1] **Rom. 3:23** For all have sinned, and come short of the glory of God.

[2] ***Rom. 5:12** Wherefore, as by one man sin entered into the world, and death by sin; and so death passed upon all men, for that all have sinned.

[3] **Titus 1:15** Unto the pure all things are pure: but unto them that are defiled and unbelieving is nothing pure; but even their mind and conscience is defiled. **Gen. 6:5** And God saw that the wickedness of man was great in the earth, and that every imagination of the thoughts of his heart was only evil continually. **Jer. 17:9** The heart is deceitful above all things, and desperately wicked: who can know it? **Rom. 3:10–19.**

3. They being the root, and by *God's* appointment, standing in the room, and stead of all mankind; the guilt of the *sin* was imputed, and *corrupted* nature conveyed, to all their posterity descending from them by ordinary generation,[1] being now conceived in *sin,*[2] and by nature children of wrath,[3] the servants of *sin,* the subjects of *death* and all other miseries, spiritual, temporal and eternal,[4] unless the *Lord Jesus* set them free.[5]

VI. OF THE FALL OF MAN

[1] **Rom. 5:12–19. 1 Cor. 15:21** For since by man came death, by man came also the resurrection of the dead. **22** For as in Adam all die, even so in Christ shall all be made alive. **45** And so it is written, The first man Adam was made a living soul; the last Adam was made a quickening spirit. **49** And as we have borne the image of the earthy, we shall also bear the image of the heavenly.

[2] **Ps. 51:5** Behold, I was shapen in iniquity; and in sin did my mother conceive me. **Job 14:4** Who can bring a clean thing out of an unclean? not one.

[3] **Eph. 2:3** Among whom also we all had our conversation in times past in the lusts of our flesh, fulfilling the desires of the flesh and of the mind; and were by nature the children of wrath, even as others.

[4] **Rom. 6:20** For when ye were the servants of sin, ye were free from righteousness. **Rom. 5:12** Wherefore, as by one man sin entered into the world, and death by sin; and so death passed upon all men, for that all have sinned.

[5] **Heb. 2:14** Forasmuch then as the children are partakers of flesh and blood, he also himself likewise took part of the same; that through death he might destroy him that had the power of death, that is, the devil. **1 Thess. 1:10** And to wait for his Son from heaven, whom he raised from the dead, even Jesus, which delivered us from the wrath to come.

4. From this original *corruption,* whereby we are utterly indisposed, disabled, and made opposite to all good, and wholly inclined to all evil,[1] do proceed all actual transgressions.[2]

[1] **Rom. 8:7** Because the carnal mind is enmity against God: for it is not subject to the law of God, neither indeed can be. **Col. 1:21**

And you, that were sometime alienated and enemies in your mind by wicked works, yet now hath he reconciled.

[2] **Jas. 1:14** But every man is tempted, when he is drawn away of his own lust, and enticed. **15** Then when lust hath conceived, it bringeth forth sin: and sin, when it is finished, bringeth forth death. **Matt. 15:19** For out of the heart proceed evil thoughts, murders, adulteries, fornications, thefts, false witness, blasphemies.

5. This *corruption* of nature, during this life, doth remain in those that are regenerated:[1] and although it be through *Christ* pardoned, and mortified, yet both itself, and the first motions thereof, are truly and properly *sin*.[2]

[1] **Rom. 7:18** For I know that in me (that is, in my flesh,) dwelleth no good thing: for to will is present with me; but how to perform that which is good I find not. **23** But I see another law in my members, warring against the law of my mind, and bringing me into captivity to the law of sin which is in my members. **Eccl. 7:20** For there is not a just man upon earth, that doeth good, and sinneth not. **1 John 1:8** If we say that we have no sin, we deceive ourselves, and the truth is not in us.

[2] **Rom. 7:24** O wretched man that I am! who shall deliver me from the body of this death? **25** I thank God through Jesus Christ our Lord. So then with the mind I myself serve the law of God; but with the flesh the law of sin. **Gal. 5:17** For the flesh lusteth against the Spirit, and the Spirit against the flesh: and these are contrary the one to the other: so that ye cannot do the things that ye would.

7

OF GOD'S COVENANT

THE DISTANCE BETWEEN *God* and the *creature* is so great, that although reasonable *creatures* do owe obedience unto him as their *Creator*, yet they could never have attained the reward of life, but by some voluntary condescension on *God's part,* which he hath been pleased to express, by way of *covenant*.[1]

> [1] **Luke 17:10** So likewise ye, when ye shall have done all those things which are commanded you, say, We are unprofitable servants: we have done that which was our duty to do. **Job 35:7** If thou be righteous, what givest thou him? or what receiveth he of thine hand? 8 Thy wickedness may hurt a man as thou art; and thy righteousness may profit the son of man.

2. Moreover *man* having brought himself under the *curse* of the law by his fall,[1] it pleased the *Lord* to make a *covenant* of *grace* wherein he freely offereth unto *sinners,* life and salvation by *Jesus Christ,* requiring of them faith in him, that they may be saved;[2] and promising to give unto all those that

are ordained unto eternal life, his Holy *Spirit,* to make them willing, and able to believe.[3]

[1] **Gen. 2:17** But of the tree of the knowledge of good and evil, thou shalt not eat of it: for in the day that thou eatest thereof thou shalt surely die. **Gal. 3:10** For as many as are of the works of the law are under the curse: for it is written, Cursed is every one that continueth not in all things which are written in the book of the law to do them. **Rom. 3:20** Therefore by the deeds of the law there shall no flesh be justified in his sight: for by the law is the knowledge of sin. **21** But now the righteousness of God without the law is manifested, being witnessed by the law and the prophets.

[2] **Rom. 8:3** For what the law could not do, in that it was weak through the flesh, God sending his own Son in the likeness of sinful flesh, and for sin, condemned sin in the flesh. **Mark 16:15** And he said unto them, Go ye into all the world, and preach the gospel to every creature. **16** He that believeth and is baptized shall be saved; but he that believeth not shall be damned. **John 3:16** For God so loved the world, that he gave his only begotten Son, that whosoever believeth in him should not perish, but have everlasting life.

[3] **Ezek. 36:26** A new heart also will I give you, and a new spirit will I put within you: and I will take away the stony heart out of your flesh, and I will give you an heart of flesh. **27** And I will put my spirit within you, and cause you to walk in my statutes, and ye shall keep my judgments, and do them. **John 6:44** No man can come to me, except the Father which hath sent me draw him: and I will raise him up at the last day. **45** It is written in the prophets, And they shall be all taught of God. Every man therefore that hath heard, and hath learned of the Father, cometh unto me. **Ps. 110:3** Thy people shall be willing in the day of thy power, in the beauties of holiness from the womb of the morning: thou hast the dew of thy youth.

VII. OF GOD'S COVENANT

3. This *covenant* is revealed in the gospel; first of all to *Adam* in the promise of salvation by the seed of the woman,[1] and afterwards by farther steps, until the full discovery thereof was completed in the New Testament;[2] and it is founded in that eternal *covenant* transaction, that was between the *Father* and the *Son,* about the redemption of the *elect;*[3] and it is alone by the grace of this *covenant,* that all of the posterity of fallen *Adam,* that ever were saved, did obtain life and a blessed immortality; *man* being now utterly uncapable of acceptance with *God* upon those terms, on which *Adam* stood in his state of innocency.[4]

[1] **Gen. 3:15** And I will put enmity between thee and the woman, and between thy seed and her seed; it shall bruise thy head, and thou shalt bruise his heel.

[2] **Heb. 1:1** God, who at sundry times and in divers manners spake in time past unto the fathers by the prophets.

[3] **2 Tim. 1:9** Who hath saved us, and called us with an holy calling, not according to our works, but according to his own purpose and grace, which was given us in Christ Jesus before the world began. **Titus 1:2** In hope of eternal life, which God, that cannot lie, promised before the world began.

[4] **Heb. 11:6** But without faith it is impossible to please him: for he that cometh to God must believe that he is, and that he is a rewarder of them that diligently seek him. **13** These all died in faith, not having received the promises, but having seen them afar off, and were persuaded of them, and embraced them, and confessed that they were strangers and pilgrims on the earth. *****Rom. 4:1** What shall we say then that Abraham our father, as pertaining to the flesh, hath found? **2** For if Abraham were justified by works, he hath whereof to glory; but not before God. **Acts 4:12** Neither is there salvation in any other: for there is

none other name under heaven given among men, whereby we must be saved. **John 8:56** Your father Abraham rejoiced to see my day: and he saw it, and was glad.

8

OF CHRIST THE MEDIATOR

IT PLEASED *God* in his eternal purpose, to choose and ordain the *Lord Jesus* his only begotten *Son,* according to the *covenant* made between them both, to be the *Mediator* between *God* and *man;*[1] the Prophet,[2] Priest[3] and King;[4] Head and Saviour of his Church, the heir of all things, and judge of the world: unto whom he did from all eternity give a people to be his seed, and to be by him in time redeemed, called, justified, sanctified, and glorified.[5]

[1] **Isa. 42:1** Behold my servant, whom I uphold; mine elect, in whom my soul delighteth; I have put my spirit upon him: he shall bring forth judgment to the Gentiles. **1 Pet. 1:19** But with the precious blood of Christ, as of a lamb without blemish and without spot: 20 Who verily was foreordained before the foundation of the world, but was manifest in these last times for you.

[2] **Acts 3:22** For Moses truly said unto the fathers, A prophet shall the Lord your God raise up unto you of your brethren, like unto me; him shall ye hear in all things whatsoever he shall say unto you.

[3] **Heb. 5:5** So also Christ glorified not himself to be made an high priest; but he that said unto him, Thou art my Son, to day

have I begotten thee. **6** As he saith also in another place, Thou art a priest for ever after the order of Melchisedec.

⁴ **Ps. 2:6** Yet have I set my king upon my holy hill of Zion. **Luke 1:33** And he shall reign over the house of Jacob for ever; and of his kingdom there shall be no end. **Eph. 1:23** Which is his body, the fulness of him that filleth all in all. **Heb. 1:2** Hath in these last days spoken unto us by his Son, whom he hath appointed heir of all things, by whom also he made the worlds. **Acts 17:31** Because he hath appointed a day, in the which he will judge the world in righteousness by that man whom he hath ordained; whereof he hath given assurance unto all men, in that he hath raised him from the dead.

⁵ **Isa. 53:10** Yet it pleased the LORD to bruise him; he hath put him to grief: when thou shalt make his soul an offering for sin, he shall see his seed, he shall prolong his days, and the pleasure of the LORD shall prosper in his hand. **John 17:6** I have manifested thy name unto the men which thou gavest me out of the world: thine they were, and thou gavest them me; and they have kept thy word. **Rom. 8:30** Moreover whom he did predestinate, them he also called: and whom he called, them he also justified: and whom he justified, them he also glorified.

2. The *Son* of *God,* the second Person in the *Holy Trinity,* being very and eternal *God,* the brightness of the Father's glory, of one substance and equal with *him:* who made the world, who upholdeth and governeth all things he hath made: did when the fullness of time was come take upon him man's nature, with all the essential properties, and common infirmities thereof,[1] yet without sin:[2] being conceived by the *Holy Spirit* in the *womb* of the *Virgin Mary,* the *Holy Spirit* coming down upon her, and the power of the most *High* overshadowing

her, and so was made of a *woman,* of the tribe of *Judah,* of the Seed of *Abraham,* and *David* according to the *Scriptures:*[3] so that two whole, perfect, and distinct natures, were inseparably joined together in one *Person:* without *conversion, composition,* or *confusion:* which *Person* is very *God,* and very *man;* yet one *Christ,* the only *Mediator* between *God* and *man.*[4]

[1] **John 1:1** In the beginning was the Word, and the Word was with God, and the Word was God. **14** And the Word was made flesh, and dwelt among us, (and we beheld his glory, the glory as of the only begotten of the Father,) full of grace and truth. **Gal. 4:4** But when the fulness of the time was come, God sent forth his Son, made of a woman, made under the law.

[2] **Rom. 8:3** For what the law could not do, in that it was weak through the flesh, God sending his own Son in the likeness of sinful flesh, and for sin, condemned sin in the flesh. **Heb. 2:14** Forasmuch then as the children are partakers of flesh and blood, he also himself likewise took part of the same; that through death he might destroy him that had the power of death, that is, the devil. **16** For verily he took not on him the nature of angels; but he took on him the seed of Abraham. **17** Wherefore in all things it behoved him to be made like unto his brethren, that he might be a merciful and faithful high priest in things pertaining to God, to make reconciliation for the sins of the people. **Heb. 4:15** For we have not an high priest which cannot be touched with the feeling of our infirmities; but was in all points tempted like as we are, yet without sin.

[3] **Luke 1:27** To a virgin espoused to a man whose name was Joseph, of the house of David; and the virgin's name was Mary. **31** And, behold, thou shalt conceive in thy womb, and bring forth a son, and shalt call his name Jesus. **35** And the angel answered and said unto her, The Holy Ghost shall come upon thee, and the power of the Highest shall overshadow thee:

therefore also that holy thing which shall be born of thee shall be called the Son of God.

⁴ **Rom. 9:5** Whose are the fathers, and of whom as concerning the flesh Christ came, who is over all, God blessed for ever. Amen. **1 Tim. 2:5** For there is one God, and one mediator between God and men, the man Christ Jesus.

3. The *Lord Jesus* in his human nature thus united to the divine, in the Person of the *Son,* was sanctified, and anointed with the *Holy Spirit,* above measure;[1] having in him all the treasures of wisdom and knowledge;[2] in whom it pleased the *Father* that all fullness should dwell:[3] to the end that being holy, harmless, undefiled,[4] and full of *grace,* and *truth,*[5] he might be throughly furnished to execute the office of a *Mediator,* and *Surety;*[6] which office he took not upon himself, but was thereunto called by his *Father;*[7] who also put all power and judgement in his hand, and gave him commandment to execute the same.[8]

[1] **Ps. 45:7** Thou lovest righteousness, and hatest wickedness: therefore God, thy God, hath anointed thee with the oil of gladness above thy fellows. **Acts 10:38** How God anointed Jesus of Nazareth with the Holy Ghost and with power: who went about doing good, and healing all that were oppressed of the devil; for God was with him. **John 3:34** For he whom God hath sent speaketh the words of God: for God giveth not the Spirit by measure unto him.

[2] **Col. 2:3** In whom are hid all the treasures of wisdom and knowledge.

[3] **Col. 1:19** For it pleased the Father that in him should all fulness dwell.

[4] **Heb. 7:26** For such an high priest became us, who is holy, harmless, undefiled, separate from sinners, and made higher than the heavens.

[5] **John 1:14** And the Word was made flesh, and dwelt among us, (and we beheld his glory, the glory as of the only begotten of the Father,) full of grace and truth.

[6] **Heb. 7:22** By so much was Jesus made a surety of a better testament.

[7] **Heb. 5:5** So also Christ glorified not himself to be made an high priest; but he that said unto him, Thou art my Son, to day have I begotten thee.

[8] **John 5:22** For the Father judgeth no man, but hath committed all judgment unto the Son. 27 And hath given him authority to execute judgment also, because he is the Son of man. **Matt. 28:18** And Jesus came and spake unto them, saying, All power is given unto me in heaven and in earth. **Acts 2:36** Therefore let all the house of Israel know assuredly, that God hath made the same Jesus, whom ye have crucified, both Lord and Christ.

4. This office the *Lord Jesus* did most willingly undertake,[1] which that he might discharge he was made under the law, and did perfectly fulfil it,[2] and underwent the punishment due to us, which we should have borne and suffered,[3] being made *sin* and a *curse* for us:[4] enduring most grievous sorrows in his soul;[5] and most painful sufferings in his body; was crucified, and died, and remained in the state of the dead; yet saw no *corruption:*[6] on the a third day he arose from the dead,[7] with the same body in which he suffered;[8] with which he also ascended into heaven:[9] and there sitteth at the right hand of *his Father,* making intercession;[10] and shall return to judge *men* and *angels,* at the end of the world.[11]

[1] **Ps. 40:7** Then said I, Lo, I come: in the volume of the book it is written of me, **8** I delight to do thy will, O my God: yea, thy law is within my heart. **Heb. 10:5–11. John 10:18** No man taketh it from me, but I lay it down of myself. I have power to lay it down, and I have power to take it again. This commandment have I received of my Father.

[2] **Gal. 4:4** But when the fulness of the time was come, God sent forth his Son, made of a woman, made under the law. **Matt. 3:15** And Jesus answering said unto him, Suffer it to be so now: for thus it becometh us to fulfil all righteousness. Then he suffered him.

[3] **Gal. 3:13** Christ hath redeemed us from the curse of the law, being made a curse for us: for it is written, Cursed is every one that hangeth on a tree. **Isa. 53:6** All we like sheep have gone astray; we have turned every one to his own way; and the LORD hath laid on him the iniquity of us all. **1 Pet. 3:18** For Christ also hath once suffered for sins, the just for the unjust, that he might bring us to God, being put to death in the flesh, but quickened by the Spirit.

[4] **2 Cor. 5:21** For he hath made him to be sin for us, who knew no sin; that we might be made the righteousness of God in him.

[5] **Matt. 26:37** And he took with him Peter and the two sons of Zebedee, and began to be sorrowful and very heavy. **38** Then saith he unto them, My soul is exceeding sorrowful, even unto death: tarry ye here, and watch with me. **Luke 22:44** And being in an agony he prayed more earnestly: and his sweat was as it were great drops of blood falling down to the ground. **Matt. 27:46** And about the ninth hour Jesus cried with a loud voice, saying, Eli, Eli, lama sabachthani? that is to say, My God, my God, why hast thou forsaken me?

[6] **Acts 13:37** But he, whom God raised again, saw no corruption.

[7] **1 Cor. 15:3** For I delivered unto you first of all that which I also received, how that Christ died for our sins according to the

VIII. OF CHRIST THE MEDIATOR

scriptures; 4 And that he was buried, and that he rose again the third day according to the scriptures.

[8] **John 20:25** The other disciples therefore said unto him, We have seen the LORD. But he said unto them, Except I shall see in his hands the print of the nails, and put my finger into the print of the nails, and thrust my hand into his side, I will not believe. 27 Then saith he to Thomas, Reach hither thy finger, and behold my hands; and reach hither thy hand, and thrust it into my side: and be not faithless, but believing.

[9] **Mark 16:19** So then after the Lord had spoken unto them, he was received up into heaven, and sat on the right hand of God. **Acts 1:9** And when he had spoken these things, while they beheld, he was taken up; and a cloud received him out of their sight. 10 And while they looked stedfastly toward heaven as he went up, behold, two men stood by them in white apparel; 11 Which also said, Ye men of Galilee, why stand ye gazing up into heaven? this same Jesus, which is taken up from you into heaven, shall so come in like manner as ye have seen him go into heaven.

[10] **Rom. 8:34** Who is he that condemneth? It is Christ that died, yea rather, that is risen again, who is even at the right hand of God, who also maketh intercession for us. **Heb. 9:24** For Christ is not entered into the holy places made with hands, which are the figures of the true; but into heaven itself, now to appear in the presence of God for us.

[11] **Acts 10:42** And he commanded us to preach unto the people, and to testify that it is he which was ordained of God to be the Judge of quick and dead. **Rom. 14:9** For to this end Christ both died, and rose, and revived, that he might be Lord both of the dead and living. 10 But why dost thou judge thy brother? or why dost thou set at nought thy brother? for we shall all stand before the judgment seat of Christ. **Acts 1:10** And while they looked

stedfastly toward heaven as he went up, behold, two men stood by them in white apparel.

5. The *Lord Jesus* by his perfect obedience and sacrifice of himself, which he through the eternal *Spirit* once offered up unto *God,* hath fully satisfied the justice of *God,*[1] procured reconciliation, and purchased an everlasting inheritance in the kingdom of heaven, for all those whom the *Father* hath given unto him.[2]

> [1] **Heb. 9:14** How much more shall the blood of Christ, who through the eternal Spirit offered himself without spot to God, purge your conscience from dead works to serve the living God? **Heb. 10:14** For by one offering he hath perfected for ever them that are sanctified. **Rom. 3:25** Whom God hath set forth to be a propitiation through faith in his blood, to declare his righteousness for the remission of sins that are past, through the forbearance of God; **26** To declare, I say, at this time his righteousness: that he might be just, and the justifier of him which believeth in Jesus.
>
> [2] **John 17:2** As thou hast given him power over all flesh, that he should give eternal life to as many as thou hast given him. **Heb. 9:15** And for this cause he is the mediator of the new testament, that by means of death, for the redemption of the transgressions that were under the first testament, they which are called might receive the promise of eternal inheritance.

6. Although the price of redemption was not actually paid by *Christ,* till after his *incarnation,* yet the virtue, efficacy, and benefit thereof were communicated to the elect in all ages

VIII. OF CHRIST THE MEDIATOR

successively, from the beginning of the world, in and by those promises, types, and sacrifices, wherein he was revealed, and signified to be the Seed of the *woman,* which should bruise the serpent's head;[1] and the Lamb slain from the foundation of the world:[2] being *the same yesterday, and to day, and for ever.*[3]

[1] **1 Cor. 4:10** We are fools for Christ's sake, but ye are wise in Christ; we are weak, but ye are strong; ye are honourable, but we are despised. **Heb. 4:2** For unto us was the gospel preached, as well as unto them: but the word preached did not profit them, not being mixed with faith in them that heard it. **1 Pet. 1:10** Of which salvation the prophets have enquired and searched diligently, who prophesied of the grace that should come unto you: 11 Searching what, or what manner of time the Spirit of Christ which was in them did signify, when it testified beforehand the sufferings of Christ, and the glory that should follow.

[2] **Rev. 13:8** And all that dwell upon the earth shall worship him, whose names are not written in the book of life of the Lamb slain from the foundation of the world.

[3] **Heb. 13:8** Jesus Christ the same yesterday, and to day, and for ever.

7. Christ in the work of *mediation* acteth according to both natures, by each nature doing that which is proper to itself; yet by reason of the unity of the person, that which is proper to one nature, is sometimes in *Scripture* attributed to the person denominated by the other nature.[1]

[1] **John 3:13** And no man hath ascended up to heaven, but he that came down from heaven, even the Son of man which is in heaven. **Acts 20:28** Take heed therefore unto yourselves, and

to all the flock, over the which the Holy Ghost hath made you overseers, to feed the church of God, which he hath purchased with his own blood.

8. To all those for whom Christ hath obtained eternal redemption, he doth certainly, and effectually apply, and communicate the same;[1] making intercession for them, uniting them to himself by his Spirit, revealing unto them, in and by the word, the mystery of salvation;[2] persuading them to believe, and obey; governing their hearts by his word and Spirit,[3] and overcoming all their enemies by his almighty power, and wisdom;[4] in such manner, and ways as are most consonant to his wonderful, and unsearchable dispensation;[5] and all of free, and absolute grace, without any condition foreseen in them, to procure it.

[1] **John 6:37** All that the Father giveth me shall come to me; and him that cometh to me I will in no wise cast out. **John 10:15** As the Father knoweth me, even so know I the Father: and I lay down my life for the sheep. **16** And other sheep I have, which are not of this fold: them also I must bring, and they shall hear my voice; and there shall be one fold, and one shepherd. **John 17:9** I pray for them: I pray not for the world, but for them which thou hast given me; for they are thine. **Rom. 5:10** For if, when we were enemies, we were reconciled to God by the death of his Son, much more, being reconciled, we shall be saved by his life.

[2] **John 17:6** I have manifested thy name unto the men which thou gavest me out of the world: thine they were, and thou gavest them me; and they have kept thy word. **Eph. 1:9** Having made known unto us the mystery of his will, according to his good pleasure which he hath purposed in himself: **1 John 5:20** And we

VIII. OF CHRIST THE MEDIATOR

know that the Son of God is come, and hath given us an understanding, that we may know him that is true, and we are in him that is true, even in his Son Jesus Christ. This is the true God, and eternal life.

[3] **Rom. 8:9** But ye are not in the flesh, but in the Spirit, if so be that the Spirit of God dwell in you. Now if any man have not the Spirit of Christ, he is none of his. 14 For as many as are led by the Spirit of God, they are the sons of God.

[4] **Ps. 110:1** The LORD said unto my Lord, Sit thou at my right hand, until I make thine enemies thy footstool. **1 Cor. 15:25** For he must reign, till he hath put all enemies under his feet. 26 The last enemy that shall be destroyed is death.

[5] **John 3:8** The wind bloweth where it listeth, and thou hearest the sound thereof, but canst not tell whence it cometh, and whither it goeth: so is every one that is born of the Spirit. **Eph. 1:8** Wherein he hath abounded toward us in all wisdom and prudence.

9. This office of Mediator between God and man, is proper only to Christ, who is the Prophet, Priest, and King of the Church of God; and may not be either in whole, or any part thereof transferred from him to any other.[1]

[1] **1 Tim. 2:5** For there is one God, and one mediator between God and men, the man Christ Jesus.

10. This number and order of offices is necessary; for in respect of our ignorance, we stand in need of his prophetical office;[1] and in respect of our alienation from God, and imperfection of the best of our services, we need his priestly office, to reconcile us, and present us acceptable unto God:[2] and in respect of our

averseness, and utter inability to return to God, and for our rescue, and security from our spiritual adversaries, we need his kingly office, to convince, subdue, draw, uphold, deliver, and preserve us to his heavenly kingdom.[3]

[1] **John 1:18** No man hath seen God at any time, the only begotten Son, which is in the bosom of the Father, he hath declared him.

[2] **Col. 1:21** And you, that were sometime alienated and enemies in your mind by wicked works, yet now hath he reconciled. **Gal. 5:17** For the flesh lusteth against the Spirit, and the Spirit against the flesh: and these are contrary the one to the other: so that ye cannot do the things that ye would.

[3] **John 16:8** And when he is come, he will reprove the world of sin, and of righteousness, and of judgment. **Ps. 110:3** Thy people shall be willing in the day of thy power, in the beauties of holiness from the womb of the morning: thou hast the dew of thy youth. **Luke 1:74** That he would grant unto us, that we being delivered out of the hand of our enemies might serve him without fear, 75 In holiness and righteousness before him, all the days of our life.

9

OF FREE WILL

GOD HATH INDUED the will of man with that natural liberty, and power of acting upon choice; that it is neither forced, nor by any necessity of nature determined to do good or evil.[1]

[1] **Matt. 17:12** But I say unto you, That Elias is come already, and they knew him not, but have done unto him whatsoever they listed. Likewise shall also the Son of man suffer of them. **Jas. 1:14** But every man is tempted, when he is drawn away of his own lust, and enticed. **Deut. 30:19** I call heaven and earth to record this day against you, that I have set before you life and death, blessing and cursing: therefore choose life, that both thou and thy seed may live.

2. Man in his state of innocency, had freedom, and power, to will, and to do that which was good, and well-pleasing to God;[1] but yet was mutable, so that he might fall from it.[2]

[1] **Eccl. 7:29** Lo, this only have I found, that God hath made man upright; but they have sought out many inventions.

[2] **Gen. 3:6** And when the woman saw that the tree was good for food, and that it was pleasant to the eyes, and a tree to be desired to make one wise, she took of the fruit thereof, and did eat, and gave also unto her husband with her; and he did eat.

3. Man by his fall into a state of sin hath wholly lost all ability of will, to any spiritual good accompanying salvation;[1] so as a natural man, being altogether averse from that good, and dead in *sin,*[2] is not able, by his own strength, to convert himself; or to prepare himself thereunto.[3]

[1] **Rom. 5:6** For when we were yet without strength, in due time Christ died for the ungodly. **Rom. 8:7** Because the carnal mind is enmity against God: for it is not subject to the law of God, neither indeed can be.

[2] **Eph. 2:1** And you hath he quickened, who were dead in trespasses and sins. 5 Even when we were dead in sins, hath quickened us together with Christ, (by grace ye are saved).

[3] **Titus 3:3** For we ourselves also were sometimes foolish, disobedient, deceived, serving divers lusts and pleasures, living in malice and envy, hateful, and hating one another. 4 But after that the kindness and love of God our Saviour toward man appeared, 5 Not by works of righteousness which we have done, but according to his mercy he saved us, by the washing of regeneration, and renewing of the Holy Ghost. **John 6:44** No man can come to me, except the Father which hath sent me draw him: and I will raise him up at the last day.

4. When God converts a sinner, and translates him into the state of grace he freeth him from his natural bondage under

IX. OF FREE WILL

sin,[1] and by his grace alone, enables him freely to will, and to do that which is spiritually good;[2] yet so as that by reason of his remaining corruptions he doth not perfectly nor only will that which is good; but doth also will that which is evil.[3]

[1] **Col. 1:13** Who hath delivered us from the power of darkness, and hath translated us into the kingdom of his dear Son. **John 8:36** If the Son therefore shall make you free, ye shall be free indeed.

[2] **Phil. 2:13** For it is God which worketh in you both to will and to do of his good pleasure.

[3] **Rom. 7:15** For that which I do I allow not: for what I would, that do I not; but what I hate, that do I. **18** For I know that in me (that is, in my flesh,) dwelleth no good thing: for to will is present with me; but how to perform that which is good I find not. **19** For the good that I would I do not: but the evil which I would not, that I do. **21** I find then a law, that, when I would do good, evil is present with me. **23** But I see another law in my members, warring against the law of my mind, and bringing me into captivity to the law of sin which is in my members.

5. The will of man is made perfectly, and immutably free to good alone, in the state of glory only.[1]

[1] **Eph. 4:13** Till we all come in the unity of the faith, and of the knowledge of the Son of God, unto a perfect man, unto the measure of the stature of the fulness of Christ.

10

OF EFFECTUAL CALLING

THOSE WHOM GOD hath predestinated unto life, he is pleased in his appointed, and accepted time, effectually to call[1] by his word, and Spirit, out of that state of sin, and death, in which they are by nature, to grace and salvation by Jesus Christ;[2] enlightening their minds, spiritually, and savingly to understand the things of God;[3] taking away their heart of stone, and giving unto them an heart of flesh;[4] renewing their wills, and by his almighty power determining them to that which is good, and effectually drawing them to Jesus Christ;[5] yet so as they come most freely, being made willing by his grace.[6]

[1] **Rom. 8:30** Moreover whom he did predestinate, them he also called: and whom he called, them he also justified: and whom he justified, them he also glorified. **Rom. 11:7** What then? Israel hath not obtained that which he seeketh for; but the election hath obtained it, and the rest were blinded. **Eph. 1:10** That in the dispensation of the fulness of times he might gather together in one all things in Christ, both which are in heaven, and which are on earth; even in him: 11 In whom also we have obtained an inheritance,

being predestinated according to the purpose of him who worketh all things after the counsel of his own will. *2 Thess. 2:13 But we are bound to give thanks alway to God for you, brethren beloved of the Lord, because God hath from the beginning chosen you to salvation through sanctification of the Spirit and belief of the truth: 14 Whereunto he called you by our gospel, to the obtaining of the glory of our Lord Jesus Christ.

[2] **Eph. 2:1–6.**

[3] **Acts 26:18** To open their eyes, and to turn them from darkness to light, and from the power of Satan unto God, that they may receive forgiveness of sins, and inheritance among them which are sanctified by faith that is in me. **Eph. 1:17** That the God of our Lord Jesus Christ, the Father of glory, may give unto you the spirit of wisdom and revelation in the knowledge of him: 18 The eyes of your understanding being enlightened; that ye may know what is the hope of his calling, and what the riches of the glory of his inheritance in the saints.

[4] **Ezek. 36:26** A new heart also will I give you, and a new spirit will I put within you: and I will take away the stony heart out of your flesh, and I will give you an heart of flesh.

[5] **Deut. 30:6** And the LORD thy God will circumcise thine heart, and the heart of thy seed, to love the LORD thy God with all thine heart, and with all thy soul, that thou mayest live. **Ezek. 36:27** And I will put my spirit within you, and cause you to walk in my statutes, and ye shall keep my judgments, and do them. **Eph. 1:19** And what is the exceeding greatness of his power to us-ward who believe, according to the working of his mighty power.

[6] **Ps. 110:3** Thy people shall be willing in the day of thy power, in the beauties of holiness from the womb of the morning: thou hast the dew of thy youth. **Song 1:4** Draw me, we will run after

X. OF EFFECTUAL CALLING

thee: the king hath brought me into his chambers: we will be glad and rejoice in thee, we will remember thy love more than wine: the upright love thee.

2. This effectual call is of God's free, and special grace alone, not from any thing at all foreseen in man, nor from any power, or agency in the creature, co-working with his special grace,[1] the creature being wholly passive therein, being dead in sins and trespasses, until being quickened and renewed by the Holy Spirit, he is thereby enabled to answer this call, and to embrace the grace offered and conveyed in it;[2] and that by no less power, than that which raised up Christ from the dead.[3]

[1] **2 Tim. 1:9** Who hath saved us, and called us with an holy calling, not according to our works, but according to his own purpose and grace, which was given us in Christ Jesus before the world began. **Eph. 2:8** For by grace are ye saved through faith; and that not of yourselves: it is the gift of God.

[2] **1 Cor. 2:14** But the natural man receiveth not the things of the Spirit of God: for they are foolishness unto him: neither can he know them, because they are spiritually discerned. **Eph. 2:5** Even when we were dead in sins, hath quickened us together with Christ, (by grace ye are saved). **John 5:25** Verily, verily, I say unto you, The hour is coming, and now is, when the dead shall hear the voice of the Son of God: and they that hear shall live.

[3] **Eph. 1:19** And what is the exceeding greatness of his power to us-ward who believe, according to the working of his mighty power, 20 Which he wrought in Christ, when he raised him from the dead, and set him at his own right hand in the heavenly places.

3. Elect infants dying in infancy are regenerated and saved by Christ through the Spirit;[1] who worketh when, and where, and how he pleaseth:[2] so also are all other elect persons, who are incapable of being outwardly called by the ministry of the word.

[1] **John 3:3** Jesus answered and said unto him, Verily, verily, I say unto thee, Except a man be born again, he cannot see the kingdom of God. **5** Jesus answered, Verily, verily, I say unto thee, Except a man be born of water and of the Spirit, he cannot enter into the kingdom of God. **6** That which is born of the flesh is flesh; and that which is born of the Spirit is spirit.

[2] **John 3:8** The wind bloweth where it listeth, and thou hearest the sound thereof, but canst not tell whence it cometh, and whither it goeth: so is every one that is born of the Spirit.

4. Others not elected, although they may be called by the ministry of the word, and may have some common operations of the Spirit,[1] yet not being effectually drawn by the Father, they neither will, nor can truly come to Christ;[2] and therefore cannot be saved: much less can men that receive not the Christian religion be saved; be they never so diligent to frame their lives according to the light of nature, and the law of that religion they do profess.[3]

[1] **Matt. 22:14** For many are called, but few are chosen. **Matt. 13:20** But he that received the seed into stony places, the same is he that heareth the word, and anon with joy receiveth it; **21** Yet hath he not root in himself, but dureth for a while: for when tribulation or persecution ariseth because of the word, by and by he is offended. **Heb. 6:4** For it is impossible for those who were once

enlightened, and have tasted of the heavenly gift, and were made partakers of the Holy Ghost, 5 And have tasted the good word of God, and the powers of the world to come.

² **John 6:44** No man can come to me, except the Father which hath sent me draw him: and I will raise him up at the last day. 45 It is written in the prophets, And they shall be all taught of God. Every man therefore that hath heard, and hath learned of the Father, cometh unto me. 65 And he said, Therefore said I unto you, that no man can come unto me, except it were given unto him of my Father. **1 John 2:24** Let that therefore abide in you, which ye have heard from the beginning. If that which ye have heard from the beginning shall remain in you, ye also shall continue in the Son, and in the Father. 25 And this is the promise that he hath promised us, even eternal life.

³ **Acts 4:12** Neither is there salvation in any other: for there is none other name under heaven given among men, whereby we must be saved. **John 4:22** Ye worship ye know not what: we know what we worship: for salvation is of the Jews. **John 17:3** And this is life eternal, that they might know thee the only true God, and Jesus Christ, whom thou hast sent.

11

OF JUSTIFICATION

THOSE WHOM GOD effectually calleth, he also freely justifieth,[1] not by infusing righteousness into them, but by pardoning their sins,[2] and by accounting, and accepting their persons as righteous;[3] not for any thing wrought in them, or done by them, but for Christ's sake alone, not by imputing faith itself, the act of believing, or any other evangelical obedience to them, as their righteousness;[4] but by imputing Christ's active obedience unto the whole law, and passive obedience in his death, for their whole and sole righteousness, they receiving, and resting on him, and his righteousness, by faith; which faith they have not of themselves, it is the gift of *God*.[5]

[1] **Rom. 3:24** Being justified freely by his grace through the redemption that is in Christ Jesus. **Rom. 8:30** Moreover whom he did predestinate, them he also called: and whom he called, them he also justified: and whom he justified, them he also glorified.

[2] **Rom. 4:5** But to him that worketh not, but believeth on him that justifieth the ungodly, his faith is counted for righteousness. **6** Even as David also describeth the blessedness of the man, unto whom God imputeth righteousness without works, **7** Saying,

Blessed are they whose iniquities are forgiven, and whose sins are covered. 8 Blessed is the man to whom the Lord will not impute sin. **Eph.** 1:7 In whom we have redemption through his blood, the forgiveness of sins, according to the riches of his grace.

³ **1 Cor.** 1:30 But of him are ye in Christ Jesus, who of God is made unto us wisdom, and righteousness, and sanctification, and redemption: 31 That, according as it is written, He that glorieth, let him glory in the Lord. **Rom.** 5:17 For if by one man's offence death reigned by one; much more they which receive abundance of grace and of the gift of righteousness shall reign in life by one, Jesus Christ. 18 Therefore as by the offence of one judgment came upon all men to condemnation; even so by the righteousness of one the free gift came upon all men unto justification of life. 19 For as by one man's disobedience many were made sinners, so by the obedience of one shall many be made righteous.

⁴ **Phil.** 3:8 Yea doubtless, and I count all things but loss for the excellency of the knowledge of Christ Jesus my Lord: for whom I have suffered the loss of all things, and do count them but dung, that I may win Christ, 9 And be found in him, not having mine own righteousness, which is of the law, but that which is through the faith of Christ, the righteousness which is of God by faith. **Eph.** 2:8 For by grace are ye saved through faith; and that not of yourselves: it is the gift of God: 9 Not of works, lest any man should boast. 10 For we are his workmanship, created in Christ Jesus unto good works, which God hath before ordained that we should walk in them.

⁵ **John** 1:12 But as many as received him, to them gave he power to become the sons of God, even to them that believe on his name. **Rom.** 5:17 For if by one man's offence death reigned by one; much more they which receive abundance of grace and of the gift of righteousness shall reign in life by one, Jesus Christ.

XI. OF JUSTIFICATION

2. Faith thus receiving and resting on Christ, and his righteousness, is the alone instrument of justification:[1] yet it is not alone in the person justified, but is ever accompanied with all other saving graces, and is no dead faith, but worketh by love.[2]

> [1] **Rom. 3:28** Therefore we conclude that a man is justified by faith without the deeds of the law.
>
> [2] **Gal. 5:6** For in Jesus Christ neither circumcision availeth any thing, nor uncircumcision; but faith which worketh by love. **Jas. 2:17** Even so faith, if it hath not works, is dead, being alone. **22** Seest thou how faith wrought with his works, and by works was faith made perfect? **26** For as the body without the spirit is dead, so faith without works is dead also.

3. Christ by his obedience, and death, did fully discharge the debt of all those that are justified; and did by the sacrifice of himself, in the blood of his cross, undergoing in their stead, the penalty due unto them: make a proper, real and full satisfaction to *God's* justice in their behalf:[1] yet in asmuch as he was given by the Father for them, and his obedience and satisfaction accepted in their stead, and both freely, not for any thing in them;[2] their justification is only of free grace, that both the exact justice and rich grace of *God,* might be glorified in the justification of sinners.[3]

> [1] **Heb. 10:14** For by one offering he hath perfected for ever them that are sanctified. **1 Pet. 1:18** Forasmuch as ye know that ye were not redeemed with corruptible things, as silver and gold, from your vain conversation received by tradition from your fathers; **19** But with the precious blood of Christ, as of a lamb without

blemish and without spot. **Isa. 53:5** But he was wounded for our transgressions, he was bruised for our iniquities: the chastisement of our peace was upon him; and with his stripes we are healed. 6 All we like sheep have gone astray; we have turned every one to his own way; and the LORD hath laid on him the iniquity of us all.

² **Rom. 8:32** He that spared not his own Son, but delivered him up for us all, how shall he not with him also freely give us all things? **2 Cor. 5:21** For he hath made him to be sin for us, who knew no sin; that we might be made the righteousness of God in him.

³ **Rom. 3:26** To declare, I say, at this time his righteousness: that he might be just, and the justifier of him which believeth in Jesus. **Eph. 1:6** To the praise of the glory of his grace, wherein he hath made us accepted in the beloved. 7 In whom we have redemption through his blood, the forgiveness of sins, according to the riches of his grace. **Eph. 2:7** That in the ages to come he might shew the exceeding riches of his grace in his kindness toward us through Christ Jesus.

4. God did from all eternity decree to justify all the elect,¹ and Christ did in the fullness of time die for their sins, and rise again for their justification;² nevertheless they are not justified personally until the *Holy Spirit* doth in due time actually apply *Christ* unto them.³

¹ **Gal. 3:8** And the scripture, foreseeing that God would justify the heathen through faith, preached before the gospel unto Abraham, saying, In thee shall all nations be blessed. **1 Pet. 1:2** Elect according to the foreknowledge of God the Father, through sanctification of the Spirit, unto obedience and sprinkling of the blood of Jesus Christ: Grace unto you, and peace, be multiplied.

XI. OF JUSTIFICATION

1 Tim. 2:6 Who gave himself a ransom for all, to be testified in due time.

[2] **Rom. 4:25** Who was delivered for our offences, and was raised again for our justification.

[3] **Col. 1:21** And you, that were sometime alienated and enemies in your mind by wicked works, yet now hath he reconciled 22 In the body of his flesh through death, to present you holy and unblameable and unreproveable in his sight. **Titus 3:4** But after that the kindness and love of God our Saviour toward man appeared, 5 Not by works of righteousness which we have done, but according to his mercy he saved us, by the washing of regeneration, and renewing of the Holy Ghost; 6 Which he shed on us abundantly through Jesus Christ our Saviour; 7 That being justified by his grace, we should be made heirs according to the hope of eternal life.

5. God doth continue to forgive the sins of those that are justified,[1] and although they can never fall from the state of justification;[2] yet they may by their sins fall under *God's* fatherly displeasure;[3] and in that condition, they have not usually the light of his countenance restored unto them, until they humble themselves, confess their sins, beg pardon, and renew their faith, and repentance.[4]

[1] **Matt. 6:12** And forgive us our debts, as we forgive our debtors. **1 John 1:7** But if we walk in the light, as he is in the light, we have fellowship one with another, and the blood of Jesus Christ his Son cleanseth us from all sin. 9 If we confess our sins, he is faithful and just to forgive us our sins, and to cleanse us from all unrighteousness.

[2] **John 10:28** And I give unto them eternal life; and they shall never perish, neither shall any man pluck them out of my hand.

³ **Ps. 89:31** If they break my statutes, and keep not my commandments; **32** Then will I visit their transgression with the rod, and their iniquity with stripes. **33** Nevertheless my lovingkindness will I not utterly take from him, nor suffer my faithfulness to fail.

⁴ **Ps. 32:5** I acknowledge my sin unto thee, and mine iniquity have I not hid. I said, I will confess my transgressions unto the LORD; and thou forgavest the iniquity of my sin. Selah. **Ps. 51**. **Matt. 26:75** And Peter remembered the word of Jesus, which said unto him, Before the cock crow, thou shalt deny me thrice. And he went out, and wept bitterly.

6. The justification of believers under the Old Testament was in all these respects, one and the same with the justification of believers under the New Testament.[1]

¹ **Gal. 3:9** So then they which be of faith are blessed with faithful Abraham. **Rom. 4:22** And therefore it was imputed to him for righteousness. **23** Now it was not written for his sake alone, that it was imputed to him; **24** But for us also, to whom it shall be imputed, if we believe on him that raised up Jesus our Lord from the dead.

12

OF ADOPTION

ALL THOSE THAT are justified, *God* vouchsafed, in, and for the sake of his only *Son Jesus Christ,* to make partakers of the grace of adoption;[1] by which they are taken into the number, and enjoy the liberties, and privileges of children of *God;*[2] have his name put upon them,[3] receive the *Spirit* of *adoption,*[4] have access to the throne of grace with boldness, are enabled to cry Abba Father,[5] are pitied,[6] protected,[7] provided for,[8] and chastened by him, as by a Father;[9] yet never cast off;[10] but sealed to the day of redemption,[11] and inherit the promises, as heirs, of everlasting salvation.[12]

[1] **Eph. 1:5** Having predestinated us unto the adoption of children by Jesus Christ to himself, according to the good pleasure of his will. **Gal. 4:4** But when the fulness of the time was come, God sent forth his Son, made of a woman, made under the law, 5 To redeem them that were under the law, that we might receive the adoption of sons.

[2] **John 1:12** But as many as received him, to them gave he power to become the sons of God, even to them that believe on his name. **Rom. 8:17** And if children, then heirs; heirs of God, and joint-heirs with Christ; if so be that we suffer with him, that we may be also glorified together.

³ **2 Cor. 6:18** And will be a Father unto you, and ye shall be my sons and daughters, saith the Lord Almighty. **Rev. 3:12** Him that overcometh will I make a pillar in the temple of my God, and he shall go no more out: and I will write upon him the name of my God, and the name of the city of my God, which is new Jerusalem, which cometh down out of heaven from my God: and I will write upon him my new name.

⁴ **Rom. 8:15** For ye have not received the spirit of bondage again to fear; but ye have received the Spirit of adoption, whereby we cry, Abba, Father.

⁵ **Gal. 4:6** And because ye are sons, God hath sent forth the Spirit of his Son into your hearts, crying, Abba, Father. **Eph. 2:18** For through him we both have access by one Spirit unto the Father.

⁶ **Ps. 103:13** Like as a father pitieth his children, so the LORD pitieth them that fear him.

⁷ **Prov. 14:26** In the fear of the LORD is strong confidence: and his children shall have a place of refuge.

⁸ **1 Pet. 5:7** Casting all your care upon him; for he careth for you.

⁹ **Heb. 12:6** For whom the Lord loveth he chasteneth, and scourgeth every son whom he receiveth.

¹⁰ **Isa. 54:8** In a little wrath I hid my face from thee for a moment; but with everlasting kindness will I have mercy on thee, saith the LORD thy Redeemer. 9 For this is as the waters of Noah unto me: for as I have sworn that the waters of Noah should no more go over the earth; so have I sworn that I would not be wroth with thee, nor rebuke thee. **Lam. 3:31** For the LORD will not cast off for ever.

¹¹ **Eph. 4:30** And grieve not the holy Spirit of God, whereby ye are sealed unto the day of redemption.

¹² **Heb. 1:14** Are they not all ministering spirits, sent forth to minister for them who shall be heirs of salvation? **Heb. 6:12** That ye be not slothful, but followers of them who through faith and patience inherit the promises.

13

OF SANCTIFICATION

THEY WHO ARE united to *Christ,* effectually called, and regenerated, having a new heart, and a new *Spirit created* in them, through the virtue of *Christ's* death, and resurrection; are also a farther sanctified,[1] really, and personally, through the same virtue, by his word and *Spirit* dwelling in them;[2] the dominion of the whole body of sin is destroyed,[3] and the several lusts thereof are more and more weakened, and mortified;[4] and they more and more quickened, and strengthened in all saving graces,[5] to the practice of all true holiness, without which no man shall see the Lord.[6]

[1] **Acts 20:32** And now, brethren, I commend you to God, and to the word of his grace, which is able to build you up, and to give you an inheritance among all them which are sanctified. **Rom. 6:5** For if we have been planted together in the likeness of his death, we shall be also in the likeness of his resurrection: **6** Knowing this, that our old man is crucified with him, that the body of sin might be destroyed, that henceforth we should not serve sin.

[2] **John 17:17** Sanctify them through thy truth: thy word is truth. **Eph. 3:16** That he would grant you, according to the

riches of his glory, to be strengthened with might by his Spirit in the inner man; **17** That Christ may dwell in your hearts by faith; that ye, being rooted and grounded in love, **18** May be able to comprehend with all saints what is the breadth, and length, and depth, and height; **19** And to know the love of Christ, which passeth knowledge, that ye might be filled with all the fulness of God. **1 Thess. 5:21** Prove all things; hold fast that which is good. **22** Abstain from all appearance of evil. **23** And the very God of peace sanctify you wholly; and I pray God your whole spirit and soul and body be preserved blameless unto the coming of our Lord Jesus Christ.

[3] **Rom. 6:14** For sin shall not have dominion over you: for ye are not under the law, but under grace.

[4] **Gal. 5:24** And they that are Christ's have crucified the flesh with the affections and lusts.

[5] **Col. 1:11** Strengthened with all might, according to his glorious power, unto all patience and longsuffering with joyfulness.

[6] **2 Cor. 7:1** Having therefore these promises, dearly beloved, let us cleanse ourselves from all filthiness of the flesh and spirit, perfecting holiness in the fear of God. **Heb. 12:14** Follow peace with all men, and holiness, without which no man shall see the Lord.

2. This sanctification is throughout, in the whole man,[1] yet imperfect in this life;[2] there abideth still some remnants of *corruption* in every part, whence ariseth a continual, and irreconcilable war; the flesh lusting against the Spirit, and the Spirit against the flesh.[3]

[1] **1 Thess. 5:23** And the very God of peace sanctify you wholly; and I pray God your whole spirit and soul and body be preserved blameless unto the coming of our Lord Jesus Christ.

XIII. OF SANCTIFICATION

[2] **Rom. 7:18** For I know that in me (that is, in my flesh,) dwelleth no good thing: for to will is present with me; but how to perform that which is good I find not. **23** But I see another law in my members, warring against the law of my mind, and bringing me into captivity to the law of sin which is in my members.

[3] **Gal. 5:17** For the flesh lusteth against the Spirit, and the Spirit against the flesh: and these are contrary the one to the other: so that ye cannot do the things that ye would. **1 Pet. 2:11** Dearly beloved, I beseech you as strangers and pilgrims, abstain from fleshly lusts, which war against the soul.

3. In which war, although the remaining *corruption* for a time may much prevail;[1] yet through the continual supply of strength from the sanctifying *Spirit* of *Christ* the regenerate part doth overcome;[2] and so the saints grow in grace, perfecting holiness in the fear of God, pressing after an heavenly life, in evangelical obedience to all the commands which *Christ* as *Head* and *King*, in his *word* hath prescribed to them.[3]

[1] **Rom. 7:23** But I see another law in my members, warring against the law of my mind, and bringing me into captivity to the law of sin which is in my members.

[2] **Rom. 6:14** For sin shall not have dominion over you: for ye are not under the law, but under grace.

[3] **Eph. 4:15** But speaking the truth in love, may grow up into him in all things, which is the head, even Christ: **16** From whom the whole body fitly joined together and compacted by that which every joint supplieth, according to the effectual working in the measure of every part, maketh increase of the body unto the edifying of itself in love. **2 Cor. 3:18** But we all, with open face beholding as in a glass the glory of the Lord, are changed into the

same image from glory to glory, even as by the Spirit of the Lord. **2 Cor. 7:1** Having therefore these promises, dearly beloved, let us cleanse ourselves from all filthiness of the flesh and spirit, perfecting holiness in the fear of God.

14

OF SAVING FAITH

THE GRACE OF *faith,* whereby the elect are enabled to believe to the saving of their souls, is the work of the *Spirit* of *Christ* in their hearts;[1] and is ordinarily wrought by the ministry of the word;[2] by which also, and by the administration of *baptism,* and the *Lord's supper, prayer* and other *means* appointed of *God,* it is increased, and strengthened.[3]

[1] **2 Cor. 4:13** We having the same spirit of faith, according as it is written, I believed, and therefore have I spoken; we also believe, and therefore speak. **Eph. 2:8** For by grace are ye saved through faith; and that not of yourselves: it is the gift of God.

[2] **Rom. 10:14** How then shall they call on him in whom they have not believed? and how shall they believe in him of whom they have not heard? and how shall they hear without a preacher? **17** So then faith cometh by hearing, and hearing by the word of God.

[3] **Luke 17:5** And the apostles said unto the Lord, Increase our faith. **1 Pet. 2:2** As newborn babes, desire the sincere milk of the word, that ye may grow thereby. **Acts 20:32** And now, brethren, I commend you to God, and to the word of his grace, which is able to build you up, and to give you an inheritance among all them which are sanctified.

2. By this *faith,* a Christian believeth to be true, whatsoever is revealed in the *word,* for the authority of *God* himself;[1] and also apprehendeth an excellency therein, above all other *writings;*[2] and all things in the *world:* as it bears forth the glory of *God* in his *attributes,* the excellency of *Christ* in his nature and offices; and the power and fullness of the *Holy Spirit* in his workings, and operations; and so is enabled to cast his soul upon the truth thus believed;[3] and also acteth differently, upon that which each particular passage thereof containeth; yielding obedience to the commands,[4] trembling at the threatenings,[5] and embracing the promises of *God,* for this life, and that which is to come:[6] but the principal acts of saving faith have immediate relation to *Christ,* accepting, receiving, and resting upon him alone, for justification, sanctification, and eternal life, by virtue of the covenant of grace.[7]

[1] **Acts 24:14** But this I confess unto thee, that after the way which they call heresy, so worship I the God of my fathers, believing all things which are written in the law and in the prophets.

[2] **Ps. 19:7** The law of the LORD is perfect, converting the soul: the testimony of the LORD is sure, making wise the simple. **8** The statutes of the LORD are right, rejoicing the heart: the commandment of the LORD is pure, enlightening the eyes. **9** The fear of the LORD is clean, enduring for ever: the judgments of the LORD are true and righteous altogether. **10** More to be desired are they than gold, yea, than much fine gold: sweeter also than honey and the honeycomb. **Ps. 119:72** The law of thy mouth is better unto me than thousands of gold and silver.

[3] **2 Tim. 1:12** For the which cause I also suffer these things: nevertheless I am not ashamed: for I know whom I have believed, and am persuaded that he is able to keep that which I have committed unto him against that day.

XIV. OF SAVING FAITH

⁴ **John 15:14** Ye are my friends, if ye do whatsoever I command you.

⁵ **Isa. 66:2** For all those things hath mine hand made, and all those things have been, saith the LORD: but to this man will I look, even to him that is poor and of a contrite spirit, and trembleth at my word.

⁶ **Heb. 11:13** These all died in faith, not having received the promises, but having seen them afar off, and were persuaded of them, and embraced them, and confessed that they were strangers and pilgrims on the earth.

⁷ **John 1:12** But as many as received him, to them gave he power to become the sons of God, even to them that believe on his name. **Acts 16:31** And they said, Believe on the Lord Jesus Christ, and thou shalt be saved, and thy house. **Gal. 2:20** I am crucified with Christ: nevertheless I live; yet not I, but Christ liveth in me: and the life which I now live in the flesh I live by the faith of the Son of God, who loved me, and gave himself for me. **Acts 15:11** But we believe that through the grace of the LORD Jesus Christ we shall be saved, even as they.

3. This *faith* although it be different in degrees, and may be weak, or strong;[1] yet it is in the least degree of it, different in the kind, or nature of it (as is all other saving grace) from the faith, and common grace of temporary believers;[2] and therefore though it may be many times assailed, and weakened; yet it gets the victory;[3] growing up in many, to the attainment of a full assurance through *Christ*,[4] who is both the author and finisher of our *faith*.[5]

[1] **Heb. 5:13** For every one that useth milk is unskilful in the word of righteousness: for he is a babe. **14** But strong meat belongeth

to them that are of full age, even those who by reason of use have their senses exercised to discern both good and evil. **Matt. 6:30** Wherefore, if God so clothe the grass of the field, which to day is, and to morrow is cast into the oven, shall he not much more clothe you, O ye of little faith? **Rom. 4:19** And being not weak in faith, he considered not his own body now dead, when he was about an hundred years old, neither yet the deadness of Sarah's womb: 20 He staggered not at the promise of God through unbelief; but was strong in faith, giving glory to God.

[2] **2 Pet. 1:1** Simon Peter, a servant and an apostle of Jesus Christ, to them that have obtained like precious faith with us through the righteousness of God and our Saviour Jesus Christ.

[3] **Eph. 6:16** Above all, taking the shield of faith, wherewith ye shall be able to quench all the fiery darts of the wicked. **1 John 5:4** For whatsoever is born of God overcometh the world: and this is the victory that overcometh the world, even our faith. 5 Who is he that overcometh the world, but he that believeth that Jesus is the Son of God?

[4] **Heb. 6:11** And we desire that every one of you do shew the same diligence to the full assurance of hope unto the end: 12 That ye be not slothful, but followers of them who through faith and patience inherit the promises. **Col. 2:2** That their hearts might be comforted, being knit together in love, and unto all riches of the full assurance of understanding, to the acknowledgement of the mystery of God, and of the Father, and of Christ.

[5] **Heb. 12:2** Looking unto Jesus the author and finisher of our faith; who for the joy that was set before him endured the cross, despising the shame, and is set down at the right hand of the throne of God.

15

OF REPENTANCE UNTO LIFE AND SALVATION

SUCH OF THE elect as are converted at riper years, having sometimes lived in the state of nature, and therein served divers lusts and pleasures, *God* in their *effectual calling* giveth them repentance unto life.[1]

> [1] **Titus 3:2** To speak evil of no man, to be no brawlers, but gentle, shewing all meekness unto all men. 3 For we ourselves also were sometimes foolish, disobedient, deceived, serving divers lusts and pleasures, living in malice and envy, hateful, and hating one another. 4 But after that the kindness and love of God our Saviour toward man appeared, 5 Not by works of righteousness which we have done, but according to his mercy he saved us, by the washing of regeneration, and renewing of the Holy Ghost.

2. Whereas there is none that doth good, and sinneth not;[1] and the best of men may through the power, and deceitfulness of their corruption dwelling in them, with the prevalency of

temptation, fall into great sins, and provocations; God hath in the covenant of grace mercifully provided that believers so sinning, and falling, be renewed through repentance unto salvation.[2]

> [1] **Eccl. 7:20** For there is not a just man upon earth, that doeth good, and sinneth not.
>
> [2] **Luke 22:31** And the Lord said, Simon, Simon, behold, Satan hath desired to have you, that he may sift you as wheat: **32** But I have prayed for thee, that thy faith fail not: and when thou art converted, strengthen thy brethren.

3. This saving repentance is an evangelical grace,[1] whereby a person being by the *Holy Spirit* made sensible of the manifold evils of his sin, doth, by faith in Christ, humble himself for it, with godly sorrow, detestation of it, and self-abhorrency;[2] praying for pardon, and strength of grace, with a purpose and endeavour by supplies of the *Spirit,* to walk before God unto all well pleasing in all things.[3]

> [1] **Zech. 12:10** And I will pour upon the house of David, and upon the inhabitants of Jerusalem, the spirit of grace and of supplications: and they shall look upon me whom they have pierced, and they shall mourn for him, as one mourneth for his only son, and shall be in bitterness for him, as one that is in bitterness for his firstborn. **Acts 11:18** When they heard these things, they held their peace, and glorified God, saying, Then hath God also to the Gentiles granted repentance unto life.
>
> [2] **Ezek. 36:31** Then shall ye remember your own evil ways, and your doings that were not good, and shall lothe yourselves in your own sight for your iniquities and for your abominations.

XV. OF REPENTANCE UNTO LIFE AND SALVATION

2 Cor. 7:11 For behold this selfsame thing, that ye sorrowed after a godly sort, what carefulness it wrought in you, yea, what clearing of yourselves, yea, what indignation, yea, what fear, yea, what vehement desire, yea, what zeal, yea, what revenge! In all things ye have approved yourselves to be clear in this matter.

[3] **Ps. 119:6** Then shall I not be ashamed, when I have respect unto all thy commandments. **128** Therefore I esteem all thy precepts concerning all things to be right; and I hate every false way.

4. As repentance is to be continued through the whole course of our lives, upon the account of the body of death, and the motions thereof; so it is every man's duty to repent of his particular known sins, particularly.[1]

[1] **Luke 19:8** And Zacchaeus stood, and said unto the Lord: Behold, Lord, the half of my goods I give to the poor; and if I have taken any thing from any man by false accusation, I restore him fourfold. **1 Tim. 1:13** Who was before a blasphemer, and a persecutor, and injurious: but I obtained mercy, because I did it ignorantly in unbelief. **15** This is a faithful saying, and worthy of all acceptation, that Christ Jesus came into the world to save sinners; of whom I am chief.

5. Such is the provision which God hath made through Christ in the covenant of grace, for the preservation of believers unto salvation, that although there is no sin so small, but it deserves damnation;[1] yet there is no sin so great, that it shall bring damnation on them that repent;[2] which makes the constant preaching of repentance necessary.

[1] **Rom. 6:23** For the wages of sin is death; but the gift of God is eternal life through Jesus Christ our Lord.

[2] **Isa. 1:16** Wash you, make you clean; put away the evil of your doings from before mine eyes; cease to do evil. **18** Come now, and let us reason together, saith the Lord: though your sins be as scarlet, they shall be as white as snow; though they be red like crimson, they shall be as wool. **Isa. 55:7** Let the wicked forsake his way, and the unrighteous man his thoughts: and let him return unto the Lord, and he will have mercy upon him; and to our God, for he will abundantly pardon.

16

OF GOOD WORKS

GOOD WORKS ARE only such as God hath commanded in his holy word;[1] and not such as without the warrant thereof, are devised by men, out of blind zeal, or upon any pretence of good intentions.[2]

[1] **Mic. 6:8** He hath shewed thee, O man, what is good; and what doth the Lord require of thee, but to do justly, and to love mercy, and to walk humbly with thy God? **Heb. 13:21** Make you perfect in every good work to do his will, working in you that which is wellpleasing in his sight, through Jesus Christ; to whom be glory for ever and ever. Amen.

[2] **Matt. 15:9** But in vain they do worship me, teaching for doctrines the commandments of men. **Isa. 29:13** Wherefore the Lord said, Forasmuch as this people draw near me with their mouth, and with their lips do honour me, but have removed their heart far from me, and their fear toward me is taught by the precept of men.

2. These good works, done in obedience to God's commandments, are the fruits, and evidences of a true, and lively faith;[1]

and by them believers manifest their thankfulness,[2] strengthen their assurance,[3] edify their brethren,[4] adorn the profession of the gospel, stop the mouths of the adversaries and glorify God[5] whose workmanship they are, created in Christ Jesus thereunto,[6] that having their fruit unto holiness, they may have the end eternal life.[7]

[1] **Jas. 2:18** Yea, a man may say, Thou hast faith, and I have works: shew me thy faith without thy works, and I will shew thee my faith by my works. **22** Seest thou how faith wrought with his works, and by works was faith made perfect?

[2] **Ps. 116:12** What shall I render unto the LORD for all his benefits toward me? **13** I will take the cup of salvation, and call upon the name of the LORD.

[3] **1 John 2:3** And hereby we do know that we know him, if we keep his commandments. **5** But whoso keepeth his word, in him verily is the love of God perfected: hereby know we that we are in him. **2 Pet. 1:5–11**.

[4] **Matt. 5:16** Let your light so shine before men, that they may see your good works, and glorify your Father which is in heaven.

[5] **1 Tim. 6:1** Let as many servants as are under the yoke count their own masters worthy of all honour, that the name of God and his doctrine be not blasphemed. **1 Pet. 2:15** For so is the will of God, that with well doing ye may put to silence the ignorance of foolish men. **Phil. 1:11** Being filled with the fruits of righteousness, which are by Jesus Christ, unto the glory and praise of God.

[6] **Eph. 2:10** For we are his workmanship, created in Christ Jesus unto good works, which God hath before ordained that we should walk in them.

[7] **Rom. 6:22** But now being made free from sin, and become servants to God, ye have your fruit unto holiness, and the end everlasting life.

XVI. OF GOOD WORKS

3. Their ability to do good works is not at all of themselves; but wholly from the *Spirit* of Christ;[1] and that they may be enabled thereunto, besides the graces they have already received, there is necessary an actual influence of the same *Holy Spirit,* to work in them to will, and to do, of his good pleasure;[2] yet are they not hereupon to grow negligent, as if they were not bound to perform any duty, unless upon a special motion of the Spirit; but they ought to be diligent in stirring up the grace of God that is in them.[3]

[1] **John 15:4** Abide in me, and I in you. As the branch cannot bear fruit of itself, except it abide in the vine; no more can ye, except ye abide in me. **6** If a man abide not in me, he is cast forth as a branch, and is withered; and men gather them, and cast them into the fire, and they are burned.

[2] **2 Cor. 3:5** Not that we are sufficient of ourselves to think any thing as of ourselves; but our sufficiency is of God. **Phil. 2:13** For it is God which worketh in you both to will and to do of his good pleasure.

[3] **Phil. 2:12** Wherefore, my beloved, as ye have always obeyed, not as in my presence only, but now much more in my absence, work out your own salvation with fear and trembling. **Heb. 6:11** And we desire that every one of you do shew the same diligence to the full assurance of hope unto the end: **12** That ye be not slothful, but followers of them who through faith and patience inherit the promises. **Isa. 64:7** And there is none that calleth upon thy name, that stirreth up himself to take hold of thee: for thou hast hid thy face from us, and hast consumed us, because of our iniquities.

4. They who in their obedience attain to the greatest height which is possible in this life, are so far from being able to

superrogate, and to do more than God requires, as that they fall short of much which in duty they are bound to do.[1]

[1] **Job 9:2** I know it is so of a truth: but how should man be just with God? **3** If he will contend with him, he cannot answer him one of a thousand. **Gal. 5:17** For the flesh lusteth against the Spirit, and the Spirit against the flesh: and these are contrary the one to the other: so that ye cannot do the things that ye would. **Luke 17:10** So likewise ye, when ye shall have done all those things which are commanded you, say, We are unprofitable servants: we have done that which was our duty to do.

5. We cannot by our best works merit pardon of sin or eternal life at the hand of God, by reason of the great disproportion that is between them and the glory to come; and the infinite distance that is between us and God, whom by them we can neither profit, nor satisfy for the debt of our former sins;[1] but when we have done all we can, we have done but our duty, and are unprofitable servants; and because as they are good they proceed from his Spirit,[2] and as they are wrought by us they are defiled and mixed with so much weakness and imperfection that they cannot endure the severity of God's judgement.[3]

[1] **Rom. 3:20** Therefore by the deeds of the law there shall no flesh be justified in his sight: for by the law is the knowledge of sin. **Eph. 2:8** For by grace are ye saved through faith; and that not of yourselves: it is the gift of God: **9** Not of works, lest any man should boast. **Rom. 4:6** Even as David also describeth the blessedness of the man, unto whom God imputeth righteousness without works.

XVI. OF GOOD WORKS

[2] **Gal. 5:22** But the fruit of the Spirit is love, joy, peace, longsuffering, gentleness, goodness, faith, **23** Meekness, temperance: against such there is no law.

[3] **Isa. 64:6** But we are all as an unclean thing, and all our righteousnesses are as filthy rags; and we all do fade as a leaf; and our iniquities, like the wind, have taken us away. **Ps. 143:2** And enter not into judgment with thy servant: for in thy sight shall no man living be justified.

6. Yet notwithstanding the persons of believers being accepted through Christ, their good works also are accepted in him;[1] not as though they were in this life wholly unblameable and unreprovable in God's sight; but that he looking upon them in his Son is pleased to accept and reward that which is sincere although accompanied with many weaknesses and imperfections.[2]

[1] **Eph. 1:6** To the praise of the glory of his grace, wherein he hath made us accepted in the beloved. **1 Pet. 2:5** Ye also, as lively stones, are built up a spiritual house, an holy priesthood, to offer up spiritual sacrifices, acceptable to God by Jesus Christ.

[2] **Matt. 25:21** His lord said unto him, Well done, thou good and faithful servant: thou hast been faithful over a few things, I will make thee ruler over many things: enter thou into the joy of thy lord. **23** His lord said unto him, Well done, good and faithful servant; thou hast been faithful over a few things, I will make thee ruler over many things: enter thou into the joy of thy lord. **Heb. 6:10** For God is not unrighteous to forget your work and labour of love, which ye have shewed toward his name, in that ye have ministered to the saints, and do minister.

7. Works done by unregenerate men although for the matter of them they may be things which God commands, and of good use, both to themselves and others;[1] yet because they proceed not from a heart purified by faith,[2] nor are done in a right manner according to the word,[3] nor to a right end the glory of God;[4] they are therefore sinful and cannot please God; nor make a man meet to receive grace from God;[5] and yet their neglect of them is more sinful and displeasing to God.[6]

[1] **2 Kgs. 10:30** And the LORD said unto Jehu, Because thou hast done well in executing that which is right in mine eyes, and hast done unto the house of Ahab according to all that was in mine heart, thy children of the fourth generation shall sit on the throne of Israel. **1 Kgs. 21:27** And it came to pass, when Ahab heard those words, that he rent his clothes, and put sackcloth upon his flesh, and fasted, and lay in sackcloth, and went softly. **29** Seest thou how Ahab humbleth himself before me? because he humbleth himself before me, I will not bring the evil in his days: but in his son's days will I bring the evil upon his house.

[2] **Gen. 4:5** But unto Cain and to his offering he had not respect. And Cain was very wroth, and his countenance fell. **Heb. 11:4** By faith Abel offered unto God a more excellent sacrifice than Cain, by which he obtained witness that he was righteous, God testifying of his gifts: and by it he being dead yet speaketh. **6** But without faith it is impossible to please him: for he that cometh to God must believe that he is, and that he is a rewarder of them that diligently seek him.

[3] **1 Cor. 13:1** Though I speak with the tongues of men and of angels, and have not charity, I am become as sounding brass, or a tinkling cymbal.

[4] **Matt. 6:2** Therefore when thou doest thine alms, do not sound a trumpet before thee, as the hypocrites do in the synagogues and

XVI. OF GOOD WORKS

in the streets, that they may have glory of men. Verily I say unto you, They have their reward. 5 And when thou prayest, thou shalt not be as the hypocrites are: for they love to pray standing in the synagogues and in the corners of the streets, that they may be seen of men. Verily I say unto you, They have their reward.

⁵ **Amos 5:21** I hate, I despise your feast days, and I will not smell in your solemn assemblies. 22 Though ye offer me burnt offerings and your meat offerings, I will not accept them: neither will I regard the peace offerings of your fat beasts. **Rom. 9:16** So then it is not of him that willeth, nor of him that runneth, but of God that sheweth mercy. **Titus 3:5** Not by works of righteousness which we have done, but according to his mercy he saved us, by the washing of regeneration, and renewing of the Holy Ghost.

⁶ **Job 21:14** Therefore they say unto God, Depart from us; for we desire not the knowledge of thy ways. 15 What is the Almighty, that we should serve him? and what profit should we have, if we pray unto him? **Matt. 25:41** Then shall he say also unto them on the left hand, Depart from me, ye cursed, into everlasting fire, prepared for the devil and his angels: 42 For I was an hungred, and ye gave me no meat: I was thirsty, and ye gave me no drink: 43 I was a stranger, and ye took me not in: naked, and ye clothed me not: sick, and in prison, and ye visited me not.

17

OF PERSEVERANCE OF THE SAINTS

THOSE WHOM GOD hath accepted in the beloved, effectually called and sanctified by his *Spirit,* and given the precious faith of his elect unto, can neither totally nor finally fall from the state of grace; but shall certainly persevere therein to the end and be eternally saved, seeing the gifts and callings of God are without repentance (whence he still begets and nourisheth in them faith, repentance, love, joy, hope, and all the graces of the Spirit unto immortality),[1] and though many storms and floods arise and beat against them, yet they shall never be able to take them off that foundation and rock which by faith they are fastened upon: notwithstanding through unbelief and the temptations of Satan the sensible sight of the light and love of God may for a time be clouded, and obscured from them,[2] yet he is still the same and they shall be sure to be kept by the power of God unto salvation, where they shall enjoy their purchased possession, they being engraven upon the palm of his hands, and their names having been written in the book of life from all eternity.[3]

[1] **John 10:28** And I give unto them eternal life; and they shall never perish, neither shall any man pluck them out of my hand. **29** My Father, which gave them me, is greater than all; and no man is able to pluck them out of my Father's hand. **Phil. 1:6** Being confident of this very thing, that he which hath begun a good work in you will perform it until the day of Jesus Christ. **2 Tim. 2:19** Nevertheless the foundation of God standeth sure, having this seal, The Lord knoweth them that are his. And, Let every one that nameth the name of Christ depart from iniquity. **1 John 2:19** They went out from us, but they were not of us; for if they had been of us, they would no doubt have continued with us: but they went out, that they might be made manifest that they were not all of us.

[2] **Ps. 89:31** If they break my statutes, and keep not my commandments; **32** Then will I visit their transgression with the rod, and their iniquity with stripes. **1 Cor. 11:32** But when we are judged, we are chastened of the Lord, that we should not be condemned with the world.

[3] **Mal. 3:6** For I am the Lord, I change not; therefore ye sons of Jacob are not consumed.

2. This perseverance of the saints depends not upon their own free will; but upon the immutability of the decree of election flowing from the free and unchangeable love of God the Father;[1] upon the efficacy of the merit and intercession of Jesus Christ and union with him,[2] the oath of God,[3] the abiding of his Spirit and the seed of God within them,[4] and the nature of the covenant of grace[5] from all which ariseth also the certainty and infallibility thereof.

[1] **Rom. 8:30** Moreover whom he did predestinate, them he also called: and whom he called, them he also justified: and whom he

justified, them he also glorified. **Rom. 9:11** For the children being not yet born, neither having done any good or evil, that the purpose of God according to election might stand, not of works, but of him that calleth. **16** So then it is not of him that willeth, nor of him that runneth, but of God that sheweth mercy.

[2] **Rom. 5:9** Much more then, being now justified by his blood, we shall be saved from wrath through him. **10** For if, when we were enemies, we were reconciled to God by the death of his Son, much more, being reconciled, we shall be saved by his life. **John 14:19** Yet a little while, and the world seeth me no more; but ye see me: because I live, ye shall live also.

[3] **Heb. 6:17** Wherein God, willing more abundantly to shew unto the heirs of promise the immutability of his counsel, confirmed it by an oath: **18** That by two immutable things, in which it was impossible for God to lie, we might have a strong consolation, who have fled for refuge to lay hold upon the hope set before us.

[4] **1 John 3:9** Whosoever is born of God doth not commit sin; for his seed remaineth in him: and he cannot sin, because he is born of God.

[5] **Jer. 32:40** And I will make an everlasting covenant with them, that I will not turn away from them, to do them good; but I will put my fear in their hearts, that they shall not depart from me.

3. And though they may through the temptation of Satan and of the world, the prevalency of corruption remaining in them, and the neglect of means of their preservation fall into grievous sins, and for a time continue therein;[1] whereby they incur God's displeasure, and grieve his Holy Spirit,[2] come to have their graces and comforts impaired,[3] have their hearts hardened, and their consciences wounded, hurt, and scandalize others,[4] and bring temporal judgements upon themselves:[5] yet

they shall renew their repentance and be preserved through faith in Christ Jesus to the end.[6]

[1] **Matt. 26:70** But he denied before them all, saying, I know not what thou sayest. **72** And again he denied with an oath, I do not know the man. **74** Then began he to curse and to swear, saying, I know not the man. And immediately the cock crew.

[2] **Isa. 64:5** Thou meetest him that rejoiceth and worketh righteousness, those that remember thee in thy ways: behold, thou art wroth; for we have sinned: in those is continuance, and we shall be saved. **9** Be not wroth very sore, O Lord, neither remember iniquity for ever: behold, see, we beseech thee, we are all thy people. **Eph. 4:30** And grieve not the holy Spirit of God, whereby ye are sealed unto the day of redemption.

[3] **Ps. 51:10** Create in me a clean heart, O God; and renew a right spirit within me. **12** Restore unto me the joy of thy salvation; and uphold me with thy free spirit.

[4] **Ps. 32:3** When I kept silence, my bones waxed old through my roaring all the day long. **4** For day and night thy hand was heavy upon me: my moisture is turned into the drought of summer. Selah.

[5] **2 Sam. 12:14** Howbeit, because by this deed thou hast given great occasion to the enemies of the Lord to blaspheme, the child also that is born unto thee shall surely die.

[6] **Luke 22:32** But I have prayed for thee, that thy faith fail not: and when thou art converted, strengthen thy brethren. **61** And the Lord turned, and looked upon Peter. And Peter remembered the word of the Lord, how he had said unto him, Before the cock crow, thou shalt deny me thrice. **62** And Peter went out, and wept bitterly.

18

OF THE ASSURANCE OF GRACE AND SALVATION

ALTHOUGH TEMPORARY BELIEVERS, and other unregenerate men, may vainly deceive themselves with false hopes, and carnal presumptions, of being in the favour of God, and state of salvation, which hope of theirs shall perish;[1] yet such as truly believe in the Lord Jesus, and love him in sincerity, endeavouring to walk in all good conscience before him, may in this life be certainly assured that they are in the state of grace;[2] and may rejoice in the hope of the glory of God which hope shall never make them ashamed.[3]

[1] **Job 8:13** So are the paths of all that forget God; and the hypocrite's hope shall perish: **14** Whose hope shall be cut off, and whose trust shall be a spider's web. **Matt. 7:22** Many will say to me in that day, Lord, Lord, have we not prophesied in thy name? and in thy name have cast out devils? and in thy name done many wonderful works? **23** And then will I profess unto them, I never knew you: depart from me, ye that work iniquity.

[2] **1 John 2:3** And hereby we do know that we know him, if we keep his commandments. **1 John 3:14** We know that we have

passed from death unto life, because we love the brethren. He that loveth not his brother abideth in death. 18 My little children, let us not love in word, neither in tongue; but in deed and in truth. 19 And hereby we know that we are of the truth, and shall assure our hearts before him. 21 Beloved, if our heart condemn us not, then have we confidence toward God. 24 And he that keepeth his commandments dwelleth in him, and he in him. And hereby we know that he abideth in us, by the Spirit which he hath given us. 1 John 5:13 These things have I written unto you that believe on the name of the Son of God; that ye may know that ye have eternal life, and that ye may believe on the name of the Son of God.

[3] **Rom. 5:2** By whom also we have access by faith into this grace wherein we stand, and rejoice in hope of the glory of God. 5 And hope maketh not ashamed; because the love of God is shed abroad in our hearts by the Holy Ghost which is given unto us.

2. This certainty is not a bare conjectural, and probable persuasion, grounded upon a fallible hope; but an infallible assurance of faith[1] founded on the blood and righteousness of Christ revealed in the gospel;[2] and also upon the inward evidence of those graces of the Spirit unto which promises are made,[3] and on the testimony of the Spirit of adoption, witnessing with our spirits that we are the children of God;[4] and as a fruit thereof keeping the heart both humble and holy.[5]

[1] **Heb. 6:11** And we desire that every one of you do shew the same diligence to the full assurance of hope unto the end. 19 Which hope we have as an anchor of the soul, both sure and stedfast, and which entereth into that within the veil.

[2] **Heb. 6:17** Wherein God, willing more abundantly to shew unto the heirs of promise the immutability of his counsel, confirmed it

XVIII. OF THE ASSURANCE OF GRACE AND SALVATION

by an oath: 18 That by two immutable things, in which it was impossible for God to lie, we might have a strong consolation, who have fled for refuge to lay hold upon the hope set before us.

[3] **2 Pet. 1:4** Whereby are given unto us exceeding great and precious promises: that by these ye might be partakers of the divine nature, having escaped the corruption that is in the world through lust. 5 And beside this, giving all diligence, add to your faith virtue; and to virtue knowledge. 10 Wherefore the rather, brethren, give diligence to make your calling and election sure: for if ye do these things, ye shall never fall: 11 For so an entrance shall be ministered unto you abundantly into the everlasting kingdom of our Lord and Saviour Jesus Christ.

[4] **Rom. 8:15** For ye have not received the spirit of bondage again to fear; but ye have received the Spirit of adoption, whereby we cry, Abba, Father. 16 The Spirit itself beareth witness with our spirit, that we are the children of God.

[5] **1 John 3:1** Behold, what manner of love the Father hath bestowed upon us, that we should be called the sons of God: therefore the world knoweth us not, because it knew him not. 2 Beloved, now are we the sons of God, and it doth not yet appear what we shall be: but we know that, when he shall appear, we shall be like him; for we shall see him as he is. 3 And every man that hath this hope in him purifieth himself, even as he is pure.

3. This infallible assurance doth not so belong to the essence of faith, but that a true believer may wait long and conflict with many difficulties before he be partaker of it;[1] yet being enabled by the Spirit to know the things which are freely given him of God, he may without extraordinary revelation in the right use of means attain thereunto:[2] and therefore it is the duty of every one, to give all diligence to make their calling and

election sure, that thereby his heart may be enlarged in peace and joy in the Holy Spirit, in love and thankfulness to God, and in strength and cheerfulness in the duties of obedience, the proper fruits of this assurance;[3] so far is it from inclining men to looseness.[4]

[1] **Isa. 50:10** Who is among you that feareth the LORD, that obeyeth the voice of his servant, that walketh in darkness, and hath no light? let him trust in the name of the LORD, and stay upon his God. **Ps. 88. Ps. 77:1–12.**

[2] **1 John 4:13** Hereby know we that we dwell in him, and he in us, because he hath given us of his Spirit. **Heb. 6:11** And we desire that every one of you do shew the same diligence to the full assurance of hope unto the end: **12** That ye be not slothful, but followers of them who through faith and patience inherit the promises.

[3] **Rom. 5:1** Therefore being justified by faith, we have peace with God through our Lord Jesus Christ: **2** By whom also we have access by faith into this grace wherein we stand, and rejoice in hope of the glory of God. **5** And hope maketh not ashamed; because the love of God is shed abroad in our hearts by the Holy Ghost which is given unto us. **Rom. 14:17** For the kingdom of God is not meat and drink; but righteousness, and peace, and joy in the Holy Ghost. **Ps. 119:32** I will run the way of thy commandments, when thou shalt enlarge my heart.

[4] **Rom. 6:1** What shall we say then? Shall we continue in sin, that grace may abound? **2** God forbid. How shall we, that are dead to sin, live any longer therein? **Titus 2:11** For the grace of God that bringeth salvation hath appeared to all men, **12** Teaching us that, denying ungodliness and worldly lusts, we should live soberly, righteously, and godly, in this present world. **14** Who gave himself for us, that he might redeem us from all iniquity, and purify unto himself a peculiar people, zealous of good works.

XVIII. OF THE ASSURANCE OF GRACE AND SALVATION

4. True believers may have the assurance of their salvation divers ways shaken, diminished, and intermitted; as by negligence in preserving of it,[1] by falling into some special *sin,* which woundeth the conscience, and grieveth the *Spirit,*[2] by some sudden or vehement temptation,[3] by God's withdrawing the light of his countenance and suffering even such as fear him to walk in darkness and to have no light;[4] yet are they never destitute of the seed of God,[5] and life of faith,[6] that love of Christ, and the brethren, that sincerity of heart, and conscience of duty, out of which by the operation of the Spirit, this assurance may in due time be revived:[7] and by the which in the meantime they are preserved from utter despair.[8]

---

[1] **Song 5:2** I sleep, but my heart waketh: it is the voice of my beloved that knocketh, saying, Open to me, my sister, my love, my dove, my undefiled: for my head is filled with dew, and my locks with the drops of the night. **3** I have put off my coat; how shall I put it on? I have washed my feet; how shall I defile them? **6** I opened to my beloved; but my beloved had withdrawn himself, and was gone: my soul failed when he spake: I sought him, but I could not find him; I called him, but he gave me no answer.

[2] **Ps. 51:8** Make me to hear joy and gladness; that the bones which thou hast broken may rejoice. **12** Restore unto me the joy of thy salvation; and uphold me with thy free spirit. **14** Deliver me from bloodguiltiness, O God, thou God of my salvation: and my tongue shall sing aloud of thy righteousness.

[3] **Ps. 116:11** I said in my haste, All men are liars. **Ps. 77:7** Will the Lord cast off for ever? and will he be favourable no more? **8** Is his mercy clean gone for ever? doth his promise fail for evermore? **Ps. 31:22** For I said in my haste, I am cut off from before thine eyes: nevertheless thou heardest the voice of my supplications when I cried unto thee.

[4] **Ps. 30:7** LORD, by thy favour thou hast made my mountain to stand strong: thou didst hide thy face, and I was troubled.

[5] **1 John 3:9** Whosoever is born of God doth not commit sin; for his seed remaineth in him: and he cannot sin, because he is born of God.

[6] **Luke 22:32** But I have prayed for thee, that thy faith fail not: and when thou art converted, strengthen thy brethren.

[7] **Ps. 42:5** Why art thou cast down, O my soul? and why art thou disquieted in me? hope thou in God: for I shall yet praise him for the help of his countenance. 11 Why art thou cast down, O my soul? and why art thou disquieted within me? hope thou in God: for I shall yet praise him, who is the health of my countenance, and my God.

[8] **Lam. 3:26–31.**

19

OF THE LAW OF GOD

GOD GAVE TO *Adam* a law of universal obedience, written in his heart, and a particular precept of not eating the fruit of the tree of knowledge of good and evil;[1] by which he bound him, and all his posterity to personal entire exact and perpetual obedience;[2] promised life upon the fulfilling, and threatned death upon the breach of it, and endued him with power and ability to keep it.[3]

[1] **Gen. 1:27** So God created man in his own image, in the image of God created he him; male and female created he them. **Eccl. 7:29** Lo, this only have I found, that God hath made man upright; but they have sought out many inventions.

[2] **Rom. 10:5** For Moses describeth the righteousness which is of the law, That the man which doeth those things shall live by them.

[3] **Gal. 3:10** For as many as are of the works of the law are under the curse: for it is written, Cursed is every one that continueth not in all things which are written in the book of the law to do them. 12 And the law is not of faith: but, The man that doeth them shall live in them.

2. The same law that was first written in the heart of man, continued to be a perfect rule of righteousness after the fall;[1] and was delivered by God upon Mount *Sinai*, in ten commandments and written in two tables;[2] the four first containing our duty towards God, and the other six our duty to man.

> [1] **Rom. 2:14** For when the Gentiles, which have not the law, do by nature the things contained in the law, these, having not the law, are a law unto themselves: **15** Which shew the work of the law written in their hearts, their conscience also bearing witness, and their thoughts the mean while accusing or else excusing one another.
>
> [2] **Deut. 10:4** And he wrote on the tables, according to the first writing, the ten commandments, which the LORD spake unto you in the mount out of the midst of the fire in the day of the assembly: and the LORD gave them unto me.

3. Besides this law commonly called moral, God was pleased to give to the people of *Israel* ceremonial laws, containing several typical ordinances, partly of worship, prefiguring Christ, his graces, actions, sufferings, and benefits;[1] and partly holding forth divers instructions of moral duties,[2] all which ceremonial laws being appointed only to the time of reformation, are by Jesus Christ the true *Messiah* and only Lawgiver who was furnished with power from the Father, for that end, abrogated and taken away.[3]

> [1] **Heb. 10:1** For the law having a shadow of good things to come, and not the very image of the things, can never with those sacrifices which they offered year by year continually make the comers thereunto perfect. **Col. 2:17** Which are a shadow of things to come; but the body is of Christ.

XIX. OF THE LAW OF GOD

² **1 Cor. 5:7** Purge out therefore the old leaven, that ye may be a new lump, as ye are unleavened. For even Christ our passover is sacrificed for us.

³ **Col. 2:14** Blotting out the handwriting of ordinances that was against us, which was contrary to us, and took it out of the way, nailing it to his cross. **16** Let no man therefore judge you in meat, or in drink, or in respect of an holyday, or of the new moon, or of the sabbath days: **17** Which are a shadow of things to come; but the body is of Christ. **Eph. 2:14** For he is our peace, who hath made both one, and hath broken down the middle wall of partition between us. **16** And that he might reconcile both unto God in one body by the cross, having slain the enmity thereby.

4. To them also he gave sundry judicial laws, which expired together with the state of that people, not obliging any now by virtue of that institution; their general equity only, being of moral use.[1]

¹ **1 Cor. 9:8** Say I these things as a man? or saith not the law the same also? **9** For it is written in the law of Moses, Thou shalt not muzzle the mouth of the ox that treadeth out the corn. Doth God take care for oxen? **10** Or saith he it altogether for our sakes? For our sakes, no doubt, this is written: that he that ploweth should plow in hope; and that he that thresheth in hope should be partaker of his hope.

5. The moral law doth for ever bind all, as well justified persons as others, to the obedience thereof,[1] and that not only in regard of the matter contained in it, but also in respect of the authority of God the Creator, who gave it:[2] neither doth

Christ in the gospel any way dissolve, but much strengthen this obligation.[3]

[1] **Rom. 13:8** Owe no man any thing, but to love one another: for he that loveth another hath fulfilled the law. 9 For this, Thou shalt not commit adultery, Thou shalt not kill, Thou shalt not steal, Thou shalt not bear false witness, Thou shalt not covet; and if there be any other commandment, it is briefly comprehended in this saying, namely, Thou shalt love thy neighbour as thyself. 10 Love worketh no ill to his neighbour: therefore love is the fulfilling of the law. **Jas. 2:8** If ye fulfil the royal law according to the scripture, Thou shalt love thy neighbour as thyself, ye do well. 10 For whosoever shall keep the whole law, and yet offend in one point, he is guilty of all. 11 For he that said, Do not commit adultery, said also, Do not kill. Now if thou commit no adultery, yet if thou kill, thou art become a transgressor of the law. 12 So speak ye, and so do, as they that shall be judged by the law of liberty.

[2] **Jas. 2:10** For whosoever shall keep the whole law, and yet offend in one point, he is guilty of all. 11 For he that said, Do not commit adultery, said also, Do not kill. Now if thou commit no adultery, yet if thou kill, thou art become a transgressor of the law.

[3] **Matt. 5:17** Think not that I am come to destroy the law, or the prophets: I am not come to destroy, but to fulfil. 18 For verily I say unto you, Till heaven and earth pass, one jot or one tittle shall in no wise pass from the law, till all be fulfilled. 19 Whosoever therefore shall break one of these least commandments, and shall teach men so, he shall be called the least in the kingdom of heaven: but whosoever shall do and teach them, the same shall be called great in the kingdom of heaven. **Rom. 3:31** Do we then make void the law through faith? God forbid: yea, we establish the law.

XIX. OF THE LAW OF GOD

6. Although true *believers* be not under the law, as a covenant of *works,* to be thereby justified or condemned;[1] yet it is of great use to them as well as to others: in that, as a rule of *life*, informing them of the will of *God,* and their duty, it directs and binds them, to walk accordingly; discovering also the sinful pollutions of their natures, hearts and lives; so as examining themselves thereby, they may come to further conviction of, humiliation for, and hatred against sin;[2] together with a clearer sight of the need they have of *Christ* and the perfection of his obedience: it is likewise of use to the regenerate to restrain their corruptions, in that it forbids sin; and the threatenings of it serve to show what even their sins deserve; and what afflictions in this life they may expect for them, although freed from the curse and unallayed rigour thereof. The promises of it likewise show them God's approbation of obedience, and what blessings they may expect upon the performance thereof, though not as due to them by the law as a covenant of works; so as man's doing good and refraining from evil, because the law encourageth to the one and deterreth from the other, is no evidence of his being under the law and not under grace.[3]

---

[1] **Rom. 6:14** For sin shall not have dominion over you: for ye are not under the law, but under grace. **Gal. 2:16** Knowing that a man is not justified by the works of the law, but by the faith of Jesus Christ, even we have believed in Jesus Christ, that we might be justified by the faith of Christ, and not by the works of the law: for by the works of the law shall no flesh be justified. **Rom. 8:1** There is therefore now no condemnation to them which are in Christ Jesus, who walk not after the flesh, but after the Spirit. **Rom. 10:4** For Christ is the end of the law for righteousness to every one that believeth.

² **Rom. 3:20** Therefore by the deeds of the law there shall no flesh be justified in his sight: for by the law is the knowledge of sin. ***Rom. 7:7** What shall we say then? Is the law sin? God forbid. Nay, I had not known sin, but by the law: for I had not known lust, except the law had said, Thou shalt not covet.

³ **Rom. 6:12** Let not sin therefore reign in your mortal body, that ye should obey it in the lusts thereof. 13 Neither yield ye your members as instruments of unrighteousness unto sin: but yield yourselves unto God, as those that are alive from the dead, and your members as instruments of righteousness unto God. 14 For sin shall not have dominion over you: for ye are not under the law, but under grace. **1 Pet. 3:8–13**.

7. Neither are the aforementioned uses of the law contrary to the grace of the gospel;¹ but do sweetly comply with it; the *Spirit* of *Christ* subduing and enabling the will of man, to do that freely and cheerfully, which the will of God revealed in the law requireth to be done.²

¹ **Gal. 3:21** Is the law then against the promises of God? God forbid: for if there had been a law given which could have given life, verily righteousness should have been by the law.

² **Ezek. 36:27** And I will put my spirit within you, and cause you to walk in my statutes, and ye shall keep my judgments, and do them.

20

OF THE GOSPEL, AND OF THE EXTENT OF THE GRACE THEREOF

THE COVENANT OF works being broken by sin, and made unprofitable unto life; God was pleased to give forth the promise of *Christ*, the seed of the woman,[1] as the means of calling the elect, and begetting in them faith and repentance; in this promise, the gospel, as to the substance of it, was revealed, and therein effectual, for the conversion and salvation of sinners.[2]

[1] **Gen. 3:15** And I will put enmity between thee and the woman, and between thy seed and her seed; it shall bruise thy head, and thou shalt bruise his heel.

[2] **Rev. 13:8** And all that dwell upon the earth shall worship him, whose names are not written in the book of life of the Lamb slain from the foundation of the world.

2. This promise of *Christ*, and salvation by him, is revealed only by the word of God;[1] neither do the works of creation, or providence, with the light of nature, make discovery of

Christ, or of *grace* by him;[2] so much as in a general, or obscure way; much less that men destitute of the revelation of him by the promise, or gospel; should be enabled thereby, to attain saving faith, or repentance.[3]

> [1] **Rom. 1:17** For therein is the righteousness of God revealed from faith to faith: as it is written, The just shall live by faith.
>
> [2] **Rom. 10:14** How then shall they call on him in whom they have not believed? and how shall they believe in him of whom they have not heard? and how shall they hear without a preacher? 15 And how shall they preach, except they be sent? as it is written, How beautiful are the feet of them that preach the gospel of peace, and bring glad tidings of good things! 17 So then faith cometh by hearing, and hearing by the word of God.
>
> [3] **Prov. 29:18** Where there is no vision, the people perish: but he that keepeth the law, happy is he. **Isa. 25:7** And he will destroy in this mountain the face of the covering cast over all people, and the vail that is spread over all nations. **With Isa. 60:2** For, behold, the darkness shall cover the earth, and gross darkness the people: but the Lord shall arise upon thee, and his glory shall be seen upon thee. 3 And the Gentiles shall come to thy light, and kings to the brightness of thy rising.

3. The revelation of the gospel unto sinners, made in divers times, and by sundry parts; with the addition of promises, and precepts for the obedience required therein, as to the nations, and persons, to whom it is granted, is merely of the sovereign will and good pleasure of God;[1] not being annexed by virtue of any promise, to the due improvement of men's natural abilities, by virtue of common light received, without it; which none ever did make, or can so do:[2] and therefore in all ages the

preaching of the gospel hath been granted unto persons and nations, as to the extent, or straightening of it, in great variety, according to the counsel of the will of God.

> [1] **Ps. 147:20** He hath not dealt so with any nation: and as for his judgments, they have not known them. Praise ye the LORD. **Acts 16:7** After they were come to Mysia, they assayed to go into Bithynia: but the Spirit suffered them not.
>
> [2] *__Rom. 1:18__ For the wrath of God is revealed from heaven against all ungodliness and unrighteousness of men, who hold the truth in unrighteousness.

4. Although the gospel be the only outward means of revealing *Christ* and saving grace; and is, as such, abundantly sufficient thereunto; yet that men who are dead in trespasses may be born again, quickened or regenerated; there is moreover necessary, an effectual, insuperable work of the Holy *Spirit,* upon the whole soul, for the producing in them a new spiritual life;[1] without which no other means will effect their conversion unto God.[2]

> [1] **Ps. 110:3** Thy people shall be willing in the day of thy power, in the beauties of holiness from the womb of the morning: thou hast the dew of thy youth. **1 Cor. 2:14** But the natural man receiveth not the things of the Spirit of God: for they are foolishness unto him: neither can he know them, because they are spiritually discerned. **Eph. 1:19** And what is the exceeding greatness of his power to us-ward who believe, according to the working of his mighty power, 20 Which he wrought in Christ, when he raised him from the dead, and set him at his own right hand in the heavenly places.

[2] **John 6:44** No man can come to me, except the Father which hath sent me draw him: and I will raise him up at the last day. **2 Cor. 4:4** In whom the god of this world hath blinded the minds of them which believe not, lest the light of the glorious gospel of Christ, who is the image of God, should shine unto them. **6** For God, who commanded the light to shine out of darkness, hath shined in our hearts, to give the light of the knowledge of the glory of God in the face of Jesus Christ.

OF CHRISTIAN LIBERTY
AND LIBERTY OF CONSCIENCE

THE LIBERTY WHICH *Christ* hath purchased for believers under the gospel, consists in their freedom from the guilt of sin, the condemning wrath of God, the rigour and curse of the law;[1] and in their being delivered from this present evil world,[2] bondage to Satan,[3] and dominion of sin;[4] from the evil of afflictions;[5] the fear, and sting of death, the victory of the grave,[6] and everlasting damnation;[7] as also in their free access to God;[8] and their yielding obedience unto him not out of a slavish fear, but a Child-like love, and willing mind.[9]

All which were common also to believers under the law for the substance of them;[10] but under the New Testament, the liberty of Christians is further enlarged in their freedom from the yoke of the ceremonial law, to which the *Jewish* Church was subjected; and in greater boldness of access to the throne of grace; and in fuller communications of the free *Spirit* of God, then believers under the law did ordinarily partake of.[11]

[1] **Gal. 3:13** Christ hath redeemed us from the curse of the law, being made a curse for us: for it is written, Cursed is every one that hangeth on a tree.

[2] **Gal. 1:4** Who gave himself for our sins, that he might deliver us from this present evil world, according to the will of God and our Father.

[3] **Acts 26:18** To open their eyes, and to turn them from darkness to light, and from the power of Satan unto God, that they may receive forgiveness of sins, and inheritance among them which are sanctified by faith that is in me.

[4] **Rom. 8:3** For what the law could not do, in that it was weak through the flesh, God sending his own Son in the likeness of sinful flesh, and for sin, condemned sin in the flesh.

[5] **Rom. 8:28** And we know that all things work together for good to them that love God, to them who are the called according to his purpose.

[6] **1 Cor. 15:54** So when this corruptible shall have put on incorruption, and this mortal shall have put on immortality, then shall be brought to pass the saying that is written, Death is swallowed up in victory. 55 O death, where is thy sting? O grave, where is thy victory? 56 The sting of death is sin; and the strength of sin is the law. 57 But thanks be to God, which giveth us the victory through our Lord Jesus Christ.

[7] **2 Thess. 1:10** When he shall come to be glorified in his saints, and to be admired in all them that believe (because our testimony among you was believed) in that day.

[8] **Rom. 8:15** For ye have not received the spirit of bondage again to fear; but ye have received the Spirit of adoption, whereby we cry, Abba, Father.

[9] **Luke 1:74** That he would grant unto us, that we being delivered out of the hand of our enemies might serve him without fear, 75 In holiness and righteousness before him, all the days of our

XXI. OF CHRISTIAN LIBERTY

life. **1 John 4:18** There is no fear in love; but perfect love casteth out fear: because fear hath torment. He that feareth is not made perfect in love.

[10] **Gal. 3:9** So then they which be of faith are blessed with faithful Abraham. **14** That the blessing of Abraham might come on the Gentiles through Jesus Christ; that we might receive the promise of the Spirit through faith.

[11] **John 7:38** He that believeth on me, as the scripture hath said, out of his belly shall flow rivers of living water. **39** But this spake he of the Spirit, which they that believe on him should receive: for the Holy Ghost was not yet given; because that Jesus was not yet glorified. **Heb. 10:19** Having therefore, brethren, boldness to enter into the holiest by the blood of Jesus, **20** By a new and living way, which he hath consecrated for us, through the veil, that is to say, his flesh; **21** And having an high priest over the house of God.

2. God alone is Lord of the conscience,[1] and hath left it free from the doctrines and commandments of men, which are in any thing contrary to his word, or not contained in it.[2] So that to believe such doctrines, or obey such commands out of conscience, is to betray true liberty of conscience;[3] and the requiring of an implicit faith, and absolute and blind obedience, is to destroy liberty of conscience, and reason also.[4]

[1] **Jas. 4:12** There is one lawgiver, who is able to save and to destroy: who art thou that judgest another? **Rom. 14:4** Who art thou that judgest another man's servant? to his own master he standeth or falleth. Yea, he shall be holden up: for God is able to make him stand.

[2] **Acts 4:19** But Peter and John answered and said unto them, Whether it be right in the sight of God to hearken unto you more than unto God, judge ye. **Acts 5:29** Then Peter and the other

apostles answered and said, We ought to obey God rather than men. **1 Cor. 7:23** Ye are bought with a price; be not ye the servants of men. **Matt. 15:9** But in vain they do worship me, teaching for doctrines the commandments of men.

[3] **Col. 2:20** Wherefore if ye be dead with Christ from the rudiments of the world, why, as though living in the world, are ye subject to ordinances. **22** (Which all are to perish with the using;) after the commandments and doctrines of men? **23** Which things have indeed a shew of wisdom in will worship, and humility, and neglecting of the body: not in any honour to the satisfying of the flesh.

[4] **1 Cor. 3:5** Who then is Paul, and who is Apollos, but ministers by whom ye believed, even as the Lord gave to every man? **2 Cor. 1:24** Not for that we have dominion over your faith, but are helpers of your joy: for by faith ye stand.

3. They who upon pretence of Christian liberty do practice any sin, or cherish any sinful lust; as they do thereby pervert the main design of the grace of the gospel, to their own destruction;[1] so they wholly destroy the end of *Christian* liberty, which is, that being delivered out of the hands of all our enemies we might serve the Lord without fear in holiness, and righteousness before him, all the days of our life.[2]

[1] **Rom. 6:1** What shall we say then? Shall we continue in sin, that grace may abound? **2** God forbid. How shall we, that are dead to sin, live any longer therein?

[2] **Gal. 5:13** For, brethren, ye have been called unto liberty; only use not liberty for an occasion to the flesh, but by love serve one another. **2 Pet. 2:18** For when they speak great swelling words of vanity, they allure through the lusts of the flesh, through much

XXI. OF CHRISTIAN LIBERTY

wantonness, those that were clean escaped from them who live in error. **19** While they promise them liberty, they themselves are the servants of corruption: for of whom a man is overcome, of the same is he brought in bondage. **20** For if after they have escaped the pollutions of the world through the knowledge of the Lord and Saviour Jesus Christ, they are again entangled therein, and overcome, the latter end is worse with them than the beginning. **21** For it had been better for them not to have known the way of righteousness, than, after they have known it, to turn from the holy commandment delivered unto them.

22

OF RELIGIOUS WORSHIP, AND THE SABBATH DAY

THE LIGHT OF nature shows that there is a God, who hath lordship, and sovereignty over all; is just, good, and doth good unto all; and is therefore to be feared, loved, praised, called upon, trusted in, and served, with all the heart, and all the soul, and with all the might.[1] But the acceptable way of worshipping the true God, is instituted by himself;[2] and so limited by his own revealed will, that he may not be worshipped according to the imaginations, and devices of men, or the suggestions of Satan, under any visible representations, or any other way, not prescribed in the holy Scriptures.[3]

[1] **Jer. 10:7** Who would not fear thee, O King of nations? for to thee doth it appertain: forasmuch as among all the wise men of the nations, and in all their kingdoms, there is none like unto thee. **Mark 12:33** And to love him with all the heart, and with all the understanding, and with all the soul, and with all the strength, and to love his neighbour as himself, is more than all whole burnt offerings and sacrifices.

[2] **Deut. 12:32** What thing soever I command you, observe to do it: thou shalt not add thereto, nor diminish from it.

[3] **Exod. 20:4** Thou shalt not make unto thee any graven image, or any likeness of any thing that is in heaven above, or that is in the earth beneath, or that is in the water under the earth. **5** Thou shalt not bow down thyself to them, nor serve them: for I the LORD thy God am a jealous God, visiting the iniquity of the fathers upon the children unto the third and fourth generation of them that hate me; **6** And shewing mercy unto thousands of them that love me, and keep my commandments.

2. *Religious worship* is to be given to *God* the *Father, Son* and *Holy Spirit,* and to him alone;[1] not to *angels, saints,* or any other *creatures;*[2] and since the fall, not without a *mediator,*[3] nor in the *mediation* of any other but Christ alone.[4]

[1] **Matt. 4:9** And saith unto him, All these things will I give thee, if thou wilt fall down and worship me. **10** Then saith Jesus unto him, Get thee hence, Satan: for it is written, Thou shalt worship the Lord thy God, and him only shalt thou serve. *****John 5:23** That all men should honour the Son, even as they honour the Father. He that honoureth not the Son honoureth not the Father which hath sent him. **Matt. 28:19** Go ye therefore, and teach all nations, baptizing them in the name of the Father, and of the Son, and of the Holy Ghost.

[2] **Rom. 1:25** Who changed the truth of God into a lie, and worshipped and served the creature more than the Creator, who is blessed for ever. Amen. **Col. 2:18** Let no man beguile you of your reward in a voluntary humility and worshipping of angels, intruding into those things which he hath not seen, vainly puffed up by his fleshly mind. **Rev. 19:10** And I fell at

XXII. OF RELIGIOUS WORSHIP & THE SABBATH DAY

his feet to worship him. And he said unto me, See thou do it not: I am thy fellow-servant, and of thy brethren that have the testimony of Jesus: worship God: for the testimony of Jesus is the spirit of prophecy.

[3] **John 14:6** Jesus saith unto him, I am the way, the truth, and the life: no man cometh unto the Father, but by me.

[4] **1 Tim. 2:5** For there is one God, and one mediator between God and men, the man Christ Jesus.

3. Prayer with thanksgiving, being one special part of natural worship, is by *God* required of all men.[1] But that it may be accepted, it is to be made in the name of the Son,[2] by the help of the Spirit,[3] according to his will;[4] with understanding, reverence, humility, fervency, faith, love, and perseverance; and when with others, in a known tongue.[5]

[1] **Ps. 95:1–7. Ps. 65:2** O thou that hearest prayer, unto thee shall all flesh come.

[2] **John 14:13** And whatsoever ye shall ask in my name, that will I do, that the Father may be glorified in the Son. **14** If ye shall ask any thing in my name, I will do it.

[3] **Rom. 8:26** Likewise the Spirit also helpeth our infirmities: for we know not what we should pray for as we ought: but the Spirit itself maketh intercession for us with groanings which cannot be uttered.

[4] **1 John 5:14** And this is the confidence that we have in him, that, if we ask any thing according to his will, he heareth us.

[5] **1 Cor. 14:16** Else when thou shalt bless with the spirit, how shall he that occupieth the room of the unlearned say Amen at thy giving of thanks, seeing he understandeth not what thou sayest? **17** For thou verily givest thanks well, but the other is not edified.

4. Prayer is to be made for things lawful, and for all sorts of men living, or that shall live hereafter;[1] but not for the dead,[2] nor for those of whom it may be known that they have sinned the sin unto death.[3]

[1] **1 Tim. 2:1** I exhort therefore, that, first of all, supplications, prayers, intercessions, and giving of thanks, be made for all men; **2** For kings, and for all that are in authority; that we may lead a quiet and peaceable life in all godliness and honesty. **2 Sam. 7:29** Therefore now let it please thee to bless the house of thy servant, that it may continue for ever before thee: for thou, O Lord God, hast spoken it: and with thy blessing let the house of thy servant be blessed for ever.

[2] **2 Sam. 12:21** Then said his servants unto him, What thing is this that thou hast done? thou didst fast and weep for the child, while it was alive; but when the child was dead, thou didst rise and eat bread. **22** And he said, While the child was yet alive, I fasted and wept: for I said, Who can tell whether God will be gracious to me, that the child may live? **23** But now he is dead, wherefore should I fast? can I bring him back again? I shall go to him, but he shall not return to me.

[3] **1 John 5:16** If any man see his brother sin a sin which is not unto death, he shall ask, and he shall give him life for them that sin not unto death. There is a sin unto death: I do not say that he shall pray for it.

5. The reading of the Scriptures,[1] preaching, and hearing the word of God,[2] teaching and admonishing one another in psalms, hymns and spiritual songs, singing with grace in our hearts to the Lord;[3] as also the administration of baptism,[4] and the Lord's supper[5] are all parts of religious worship of *God,* to

XXII. OF RELIGIOUS WORSHIP & THE SABBATH DAY

be performed in obedience to him, with understanding, faith, reverence, and godly fear; moreover solemn humiliation with fastings;[6] and thanksgiving upon special occasions,[7] ought to be used in an holy and religious manner.

[1] **1 Tim. 4:13** Till I come, give attendance to reading, to exhortation, to doctrine.

[2] **2 Tim. 4:2** Preach the word; be instant in season, out of season; reprove, rebuke, exhort with all longsuffering and doctrine. **Luke 8:18** Take heed therefore how ye hear: for whosoever hath, to him shall be given; and whosoever hath not, from him shall be taken even that which he seemeth to have.

[3] **Col. 3:16** Let the word of Christ dwell in you richly in all wisdom; teaching and admonishing one another in psalms and hymns and spiritual songs, singing with grace in your hearts to the Lord. **Eph. 5:19** Speaking to yourselves in psalms and hymns and spiritual songs, singing and making melody in your heart to the Lord.

[4] **Matt. 28:19** Go ye therefore, and teach all nations, baptizing them in the name of the Father, and of the Son, and of the Holy Ghost: 20 Teaching them to observe all things whatsoever I have commanded you: and, lo, I am with you alway, even unto the end of the world. Amen.

[5] **1 Cor. 11:26** For as often as ye eat this bread, and drink this cup, ye do shew the Lord's death till he come.

[6] **Esth. 4:16** Go, gather together all the Jews that are present in Shushan, and fast ye for me, and neither eat nor drink three days, night or day: I also and my maidens will fast likewise; and so will I go in unto the king, which is not according to the law: and if I perish, I perish. **Joel 2:12** Therefore also now, saith the Lord, turn ye even to me with all your heart, and with fasting, and with weeping, and with mourning.

A CONFESSION OF FAITH

⁷ *__Exod. 15:1__ Then sang Moses and the children of Israel this song unto the LORD, and spake, saying, I will sing unto the LORD, for he hath triumphed gloriously: the horse and his rider hath he thrown into the sea. **Ps. 107.**

6. Neither *prayer*, nor any other part of religious worship, is now under the gospel tied unto, or made more acceptable by, any place in which it is performed, or towards which it is directed; but God is to be worshipped everywhere in *Spirit,* and in truth;[1] as in private families[2] daily,[3] and in secret each one by himself,[4] so more solemnly in the public assemblies, which are not carelessly, nor wilfully, to be neglected, or forsaken, when God by his word, or providence calleth thereunto.[5]

[1] **John 4:21** Jesus saith unto her, Woman, believe me, the hour cometh, when ye shall neither in this mountain, nor yet at Jerusalem, worship the Father. **Mal. 1:11** For from the rising of the sun even unto the going down of the same my name shall be great among the Gentiles; and in every place incense shall be offered unto my name, and a pure offering: for my name shall be great among the heathen, saith the LORD of hosts. **1 Tim. 2:8** I will therefore that men pray every where, lifting up holy hands, without wrath and doubting.

[2] **Acts 10:2** A devout man, and one that feared God with all his house, which gave much alms to the people, and prayed to God alway.

[3] **Matt. 6:11** Give us this day our daily bread. **Ps. 55:17** Evening, and morning, and at noon, will I pray, and cry aloud: and he shall hear my voice.

[4] **Matt. 6:6** But thou, when thou prayest, enter into thy closet, and when thou hast shut thy door, pray to thy Father which is

XXII. OF RELIGIOUS WORSHIP & THE SABBATH DAY

in secret; and thy Father which seeth in secret shall reward thee openly.

⁵ **Heb. 10:25** Not forsaking the assembling of ourselves together, as the manner of some is; but exhorting one another: and so much the more, as ye see the day approaching. **Acts 2:42** And they continued stedfastly in the apostles' doctrine and fellowship, and in breaking of bread, and in prayers.

7. As it is of the law of nature, that in general a proportion of time, by God's appointment, be set apart for the worship of God; so by his word in a positive-moral, and perpetual commandment, binding all men, in all ages, he hath particularly appointed one day in seven for a *Sabbath* to be kept holy unto him,[1] which from the beginning of the world to the resurrection of Christ, was the last day of the week; and from the resurrection of Christ, was changed into the first day of the week which is called the Lord's day;[2] and is to be continued to the end of the world, as the *Christian Sabbath;* the observation of the last day of the week being abolished.

[1] **Exod. 20:8** Remember the sabbath day, to keep it holy.

[2] **1 Cor. 16:1** Now concerning the collection for the saints, as I have given order to the churches of Galatia, even so do ye. 2 Upon the first day of the week let every one of you lay by him in store, as God hath prospered him, that there be no gatherings when I come. **Acts 20:7** And upon the first day of the week, when the disciples came together to break bread, Paul preached unto them, ready to depart on the morrow; and continued his speech until midnight. **Rev. 1:10** I was in the Spirit on the Lord's day, and heard behind me a great voice, as of a trumpet.

8. The *Sabbath* is then kept holy unto the Lord, when men after a due preparing of their hearts, and ordering their common affairs aforehand, do not only observe an holy rest all the day, from their own works, words, and thoughts, about their worldly employment, and recreations,[1] but also are taken up the whole time in the public and private exercises of his worship, and in the duties of necessity and mercy.[2]

[1] **Isa. 58:13** If thou turn away thy foot from the sabbath, from doing thy pleasure on my holy day; and call the sabbath a delight, the holy of the Lord, honourable; and shalt honour him, not doing thine own ways, nor finding thine own pleasure, nor speaking thine own words. **Neh. 13:15–22.**

[2] **Matt. 12:1–13.**

23

OF LAWFUL OATHS AND VOWS

A LAWFUL OATH IS a part of religious worship, wherein the person swearing in truth, righteousness, and judgement, solemnly calleth God to witness what he sweareth;[1] and to judge him according to the truth or falseness thereof.[2]

[1] **Exod. 20:7** Thou shalt not take the name of the LORD thy God in vain; for the LORD will not hold him guiltless that taketh his name in vain. **Deut. 10:20** Thou shalt fear the LORD thy God; him shalt thou serve, and to him shalt thou cleave, and swear by his name. **Jer. 4:2** And thou shalt swear, The LORD liveth, in truth, in judgment, and in righteousness; and the nations shall bless themselves in him, and in him shall they glory.

[2] **2 Chr. 6:22** If a man sin against his neighbour, and an oath be laid upon him to make him swear, and the oath come before thine altar in this house; **23** Then hear thou from heaven, and do, and judge thy servants, by requiting the wicked, by recompensing his way upon his own head; and by justifying the righteous, by giving him according to his righteousness.

2. The name of God only is that by which men ought to swear; and therein it is to be used, with all holy fear and reverence, therefore to swear vainly or rashly by that glorious, and dreadful name; or to *swear* at all by any other thing, is sinful and to be abhorred;[1] yet as in matter of weight and moment for confirmation of truth, and ending all strife, an *oath* is warranted by the word of God;[2] so a *lawful oath* being imposed, by lawful authority, in such matters, ought to be taken.[3]

[1] **Matt. 5:34** But I say unto you, Swear not at all; neither by heaven; for it is God's throne. 37 But let your communication be, Yea, yea; Nay, nay: for whatsoever is more than these cometh of evil. **Jas. 5:12** But above all things, my brethren, swear not, neither by heaven, neither by the earth, neither by any other oath: but let your yea be yea; and your nay, nay; lest ye fall into condemnation.

[2] **Heb. 6:16** For men verily swear by the greater: and an oath for confirmation is to them an end of all strife. **2 Cor. 1:23** Moreover I call God for a record upon my soul, that to spare you I came not as yet unto Corinth.

[3] **Neh. 13:25** And I contended with them, and cursed them, and smote certain of them, and plucked off their hair, and made them swear by God, saying, Ye shall not give your daughters unto their sons, nor take their daughters unto your sons, or for yourselves.

3. Whosoever taketh an *oath* warranted by the word of God, ought duly to consider the weightiness of so solemn an act; and therein to avouch nothing, but what he knoweth to be the truth; for that by rash, false, and vain *oaths* the Lord is provoked, and for them this land mourns.[1]

XXIII. OF LAWFUL OATHS AND VOWS

[1] **Lev. 19:12** And ye shall not swear by my name falsely, neither shalt thou profane the name of thy God: I am the Lord. **Jer. 23:10** For the land is full of adulterers; for because of swearing the land mourneth; the pleasant places of the wilderness are dried up, and their course is evil, and their force is not right.

4. An *oath* is to be taken in the plain, and common sense of the words; without equivocation, or mental reservation.[1]

[1] **Ps. 24:4** He that hath clean hands, and a pure heart; who hath not lifted up his soul unto vanity, nor sworn deceitfully.

5. A vow which is not to be made to any *creature,* but to God alone, is to be made and performed with all religious care, and faithfulness:[1] but Popish *monastical vows,* of perpetual single life,[2] professed poverty,[3] and regular obedience, are so far from being degrees of higher perfection, that they are superstitious, and sinful snares, in which no *Christian* may entangle himself.[4]

[1] **Ps. 76:11** Vow, and pay unto the Lord your God: let all that be round about him bring presents unto him that ought to be feared. **Gen. 28:20** And Jacob vowed a vow, saying, If God will be with me, and will keep me in this way that I go, and will give me bread to eat, and raiment to put on, **21** So that I come again to my father's house in peace; then shall the Lord be my God: **22** And this stone, which I have set for a pillar, shall be God's house: and of all that thou shalt give me I will surely give the tenth unto thee.

[2] **1 Cor. 7:2** Nevertheless, to avoid fornication, let every man have his own wife, and let every woman have her own husband.

9 But if they cannot contain, let them marry: for it is better to marry than to burn.

[3] **Eph. 4:28** Let him that stole steal no more: but rather let him labour, working with his hands the thing which is good, that he may have to give to him that needeth.

[4] **Matt. 19:11** But he said unto them, All men cannot receive this saying, save they to whom it is given.

24

OF THE CIVIL MAGISTRATE

G OD THE SUPREME Lord, and King of all the world, hath ordained *civil magistrates* to be under him, over the people for his own glory, and the public good; and to this end hath armed them with the power of the sword, for defence and encouragement of them that do good, and for the punishment of evil doers.[1]

[1] **Rom. 13:1** Let every soul be subject unto the higher powers. For there is no power but of God: the powers that be are ordained of God. 2 Whosoever therefore resisteth the power, resisteth the ordinance of God: and they that resist shall receive to themselves damnation. 3 For rulers are not a terror to good works, but to the evil. Wilt thou then not be afraid of the power? do that which is good, and thou shalt have praise of the same: 4 For he is the minister of God to thee for good. But if thou do that which is evil, be afraid; for he beareth not the sword in vain: for he is the minister of God, a revenger to execute wrath upon him that doeth evil.

2. It is lawful for Christians to accept and execute the office of a *magistrate,* when called thereunto; in the management whereof, as they ought especially to maintain justice, and peace, according to the wholesome laws of each kingdom, and commonwealth:[1] so for that end they may lawfully now under the New Testament wage war upon just and necessary occasions.[2]

[1] **2 Sam. 23:3** The God of Israel said, the Rock of Israel spake to me, He that ruleth over men must be just, ruling in the fear of God. **Ps. 82:3** Defend the poor and fatherless: do justice to the afflicted and needy. 4 Deliver the poor and needy: rid them out of the hand of the wicked.

[2] **Luke 3:14** And the soldiers likewise demanded of him, saying, And what shall we do? And he said unto them, Do violence to no man, neither accuse any falsely; and be content with your wages.

3. *Civil magistrates* being set up by God, for the ends aforesaid; subjection in all lawful things commanded by them, ought to be yielded by us, in the Lord; not only for wrath but for conscience' sake;[1] and we ought to make supplications and prayers for kings, and all that are in authority, that under them we may live a quiet and peaceable life, in all godliness and honesty.[2]

[1] **Rom. 13:5** Wherefore ye must needs be subject, not only for wrath, but also for conscience sake. 6 For for this cause pay ye tribute also: for they are God's ministers, attending continually upon this very thing. 7 Render therefore to all their dues: tribute to whom tribute is due; custom to whom custom; fear to whom

XXIV. OF THE CIVIL MAGISTRATE

fear; honour to whom honour. 1 **Pet. 2:17** Honour all men. Love the brotherhood. Fear God. Honour the king.

[2] **1 Tim. 2:1** I exhort therefore, that, first of all, supplications, prayers, intercessions, and giving of thanks, be made for all men; 2 For kings, and for all that are in authority; that we may lead a quiet and peaceable life in all godliness and honesty.

25

OF MARRIAGE

MARRIAGE IS TO be between one *man* and one *woman;* neither is it lawful for any man to have more then one *wife,* nor for any *woman* to have more than one *husband* at the same time.[1]

> [1] **Gen. 2:24** Therefore shall a man leave his father and his mother, and shall cleave unto his wife: and they shall be one flesh. **Mal. 2:15** And did not he make one? Yet had he the residue of the spirit. And wherefore one? That he might seek a godly seed. Therefore take heed to your spirit, and let none deal treacherously against the wife of his youth. **Matt. 19:5** And said, For this cause shall a man leave father and mother, and shall cleave to his wife: and they twain shall be one flesh? **6** Wherefore they are no more twain, but one flesh. What therefore God hath joined together, let not man put asunder.

2. Marriage was ordained for the mutual help of *husband* and *wife,*[1] for the increase of mankind, with a legitimate issue,[2] and for preventing of uncleanness.[3]

[1] **Gen. 2:18** And the LORD God said, It is not good that the man should be alone; I will make him an help meet for him.

[2] **Gen. 1:28** And God blessed them, and God said unto them, Be fruitful, and multiply, and replenish the earth, and subdue it: and have dominion over the fish of the sea, and over the fowl of the air, and over every living thing that moveth upon the earth.

[3] **1 Cor. 7:2** Nevertheless, to avoid fornication, let every man have his own wife, and let every woman have her own husband. **9** But if they cannot contain, let them marry: for it is better to marry than to burn.

3. It is lawful for all sorts of people to *marry*, who are able with judgement to give their consent;[1] yet it is the duty of *Christians* to *marry* in the Lord,[2] and therefore such as profess the true religion, should not *marry* with infidels, or idolaters; neither should such as are godly be unequally yoked, by *marrying* with such as are wicked, in their life, or maintain damnable heresy.[3]

[1] **Heb. 13:4** Marriage is honourable in all, and the bed undefiled: but whoremongers and adulterers God will judge. **1 Tim. 4:3** Forbidding to marry, and commanding to abstain from meats, which God hath created to be received with thanksgiving of them which believe and know the truth.

[2] **1 Cor. 7:39** The wife is bound by the law as long as her husband liveth; but if her husband be dead, she is at liberty to be married to whom she will; only in the Lord.

[3] **Neh. 13:25** And I contended with them, and cursed them, and smote certain of them, and plucked off their hair, and made them swear by God, saying, Ye shall not give your daughters unto their sons, nor take their daughters unto your sons, or for

yourselves. 26 Did not Solomon king of Israel sin by these things? yet among many nations was there no king like him, who was beloved of his God, and God made him king over all Israel: nevertheless even him did outlandish women cause to sin. 27 Shall we then hearken unto you to do all this great evil, to transgress against our God in marrying strange wives?

4. *Marriage* ought not to be within the degrees of consanguinity, or affinity forbidden in the word;[1] nor can such incestuous *marriage* ever be made lawful, by any law of *man* or consent of parties, so as those persons may live together as *man* and *wife*.[2]

[1] Lev. 18.

[2] ***Mark 6:18** For John had said unto Herod, It is not lawful for thee to have thy brother's wife. **1 Cor. 5:1** It is reported commonly that there is fornication among you, and such fornication as is not so much as named among the Gentiles, that one should have his father's wife.

26

OF THE CHURCH

THE CATHOLIC OR universal Church, which (with respect to the internal work of the Spirit, and truth of grace) may be called invisible, consists of the whole number of the elect, that have been, are, or shall be gathered into one, under Christ the head thereof; and is the spouse, the body, the fullness of him that filleth all in all.[1]

---

[1] **Heb. 12:23** To the general assembly and church of the firstborn, which are written in heaven, and to God the Judge of all, and to the spirits of just men made perfect. **Col. 1:18** And he is the head of the body, the church: who is the beginning, the firstborn from the dead; that in all things he might have the preeminence. **Eph. 1:10** That in the dispensation of the fulness of times he might gather together in one all things in Christ, both which are in heaven, and which are on earth; even in him. **22** And hath put all things under his feet, and gave him to be the head over all things to the church, **23** Which is his body, the fulness of him that filleth all in all. **Eph. 5:23** For the husband is the head of the wife, even as Christ is the head of the church: and he is the saviour of the body. **27** That he might present it to himself a glorious church, not having spot, or wrinkle, or any

such thing; but that it should be holy and without blemish. 32 This is a great mystery: but I speak concerning Christ and the church.

2. All persons throughout the world, professing the faith of the gospel, and obedience unto God by Christ, according unto it; not destroying their own profession by any errors everting the foundation, or unholiness of conversation, are and may be called visible saints;[1] and of such ought all particular congregations to be constituted.[2]

[1] **1 Cor. 1:2** Unto the church of God which is at Corinth, to them that are sanctified in Christ Jesus, called to be saints, with all that in every place call upon the name of Jesus Christ our Lord, both theirs and ours. **Acts 11:26** And when he had found him, he brought him unto Antioch. And it came to pass, that a whole year they assembled themselves with the church, and taught much people. And the disciples were called Christians first in Antioch.

[2] **Rom. 1:7** To all that be in Rome, beloved of God, called to be saints: Grace to you and peace from God our Father, and the Lord Jesus Christ. **Eph. 1:20** Which he wrought in Christ, when he raised him from the dead, and set him at his own right hand in the heavenly places, 21 Far above all principality, and power, and might, and dominion, and every name that is named, not only in this world, but also in that which is to come: 22 And hath put all things under his feet, and gave him to be the head over all things to the church.

3. The purest churches under heaven are subject to mixture, and error;[1] and some have so degenerated as to become no churches of Christ, but synagogues of Satan;[2] nevertheless Christ always hath had, and ever shall have a kingdom in this

XXVI. OF THE CHURCH

world, to the end thereof, of such as believe in him, and make profession of his name.[3]

[1] 1 Cor. 15. Rev. 2–3.

[2] **Rev. 18:2** And he cried mightily with a strong voice, saying, Babylon the great is fallen, is fallen, and is become the habitation of devils, and the hold of every foul spirit, and a cage of every unclean and hateful bird. **2 Thess. 2:11** And for this cause God shall send them strong delusion, that they should believe a lie: **12** That they all might be damned who believed not the truth, but had pleasure in unrighteousness.

[3] **Matt. 16:18** And I say also unto thee, That thou art Peter, and upon this rock I will build my church; and the gates of hell shall not prevail against it. **Ps. 72:17** His name shall endure for ever: his name shall be continued as long as the sun: and men shall be blessed in him: all nations shall call him blessed. **Ps. 102:28** The children of thy servants shall continue, and their seed shall be established before thee. **Rev. 12:17** And the dragon was wroth with the woman, and went to make war with the remnant of her seed, which keep the commandments of God, and have the testimony of Jesus Christ.

4. The Lord Jesus Christ is the head of the Church, in whom by the appointment of the Father, all power for the calling, institution, order, or government of the Church, is invested in a supreme and sovereign manner,[1] neither can the Pope of *Rome* in any sense be head thereof, but is that antichrist, that man of sin, and son of perdition, that exalteth himself in the Church against Christ, and all that is called God; whom the Lord shall destroy with the brightness of his coming.[2]

[1] **Col. 1:18** And he is the head of the body, the church: who is

the beginning, the firstborn from the dead; that in all things he might have the preeminence. **Matt. 28:18** And Jesus came and spake unto them, saying, All power is given unto me in heaven and in earth. 19 Go ye therefore, and teach all nations, baptizing them in the name of the Father, and of the Son, and of the Holy Ghost: 20 Teaching them to observe all things whatsoever I have commanded you: and, lo, I am with you alway, even unto the end of the world. Amen. **Eph. 4:11** And he gave some, apostles; and some, prophets; and some, evangelists; and some, pastors and teachers; 12 For the perfecting of the saints, for the work of the ministry, for the edifying of the body of Christ.

[2] 2 Thess. 2:3–9.

5. In the execution of this power wherewith he is so entrusted, the Lord Jesus calleth out of the world unto himself, through the ministry of his word, by his Spirit, those that are given unto him by his Father;[1] that they may walk before him in all the ways of obedience, which he prescribeth to them in his word.[2] Those thus called he commandeth to walk together in particular societies, or churches, for their mutual edification; and the due performance of that public worship, which he requireth of them in the world.[3]

[1] **John 10:16** And other sheep I have, which are not of this fold: them also I must bring, and they shall hear my voice; and there shall be one fold, and one shepherd. **John 12:32** And I, if I be lifted up from the earth, will draw all men unto me.

[2] **Matt. 28:20** Teaching them to observe all things whatsoever I have commanded you: and, lo, I am with you alway, even unto the end of the world. Amen.

[3] Matt. 28:15–20.

XXVI. OF THE CHURCH

6. The members of these churches are saints by calling, visibly manifesting and evidencing (in and by their profession and walking) their obedience unto that call of Christ;[1] and do willingly consent to walk together according to the appointment of Christ, giving up themselves, to the Lord and one to another by the will of God, in professed subjection to the ordinances of the gospel.[2]

[1] **Rom. 1:7** To all that be in Rome, beloved of God, called to be saints: Grace to you and peace from God our Father, and the Lord Jesus Christ. **1 Cor. 1:2** Unto the church of God which is at Corinth, to them that are sanctified in Christ Jesus, called to be saints, with all that in every place call upon the name of Jesus Christ our Lord, both theirs and ours.

[2] **Acts 2:41** Then they that gladly received his word were baptized: and the same day there were added unto them about three thousand souls. **42** And they continued stedfastly in the apostles' doctrine and fellowship, and in breaking of bread, and in prayers. **Acts 5:13** And of the rest durst no man join himself to them: but the people magnified them. **14** And believers were the more added to the Lord, multitudes both of men and women. **2 Cor. 9:13** Whiles by the experiment of this ministration they glorify God for your professed subjection unto the gospel of Christ, and for your liberal distribution unto them, and unto all men.

7. To each of these churches thus gathered, according to his mind, declared in his word, he hath given all that power and authority, which is any way needful, for their carrying on that order in worship, and discipline, which he hath instituted for them to observe; with commands, and rules, for the due and right exerting, and executing of that power.[1]

[1] **Matt. 18:17** And if he shall neglect to hear them, tell it unto the church: but if he neglect to hear the church, let him be unto thee as an heathen man and a publican. 18 Verily I say unto you, Whatsoever ye shall bind on earth shall be bound in heaven: and whatsoever ye shall loose on earth shall be loosed in heaven. **1 Cor. 5:4** In the name of our Lord Jesus Christ, when ye are gathered together, and my spirit, with the power of our Lord Jesus Christ, 5 To deliver such an one unto Satan for the destruction of the flesh, that the spirit may be saved in the day of the Lord Jesus. **With 1 Cor. 5:13** But them that are without God judgeth. Therefore put away from among yourselves that wicked person. **2 Cor. 2:6** Sufficient to such a man is this punishment, which was inflicted of many. 7 So that contrariwise ye ought rather to forgive him, and comfort him, lest perhaps such a one should be swallowed up with overmuch sorrow. 8 Wherefore I beseech you that ye would confirm your love toward him.

8. A particular church gathered, and completely organized, according to the mind of Christ, consists of officers, and members; and the officers appointed by *Christ* to be chosen and set apart by the church (so called and gathered) for the peculiar administration of ordinances, and execution of power, or duty, which he entrusts them with, or calls them to, to be continued to the end of the world are bishops or elders and deacons.[1]

[1] **Acts 20:17** And from Miletus he sent to Ephesus, and called the elders of the church. **With Acts 20:28** Take heed therefore unto yourselves, and to all the flock, over the which the Holy Ghost hath made you overseers, to feed the church of God, which he hath purchased with his own blood. **Phil. 1:1** Paul and Timotheus, the

servants of Jesus Christ, to all the saints in Christ Jesus which are at Philippi, with the bishops and deacons.

9. The way appointed by *Christ* for the calling of any person, fitted, and gifted by the Holy *Spirit*, unto the office of bishop, or elder, in a church, is, that he be chosen thereunto by the common suffrage of the church itself;[1] and solemnly set apart by fasting and prayer, with imposition of hands of the eldership of the church, if there be any before constituted therein;[2] and of a deacon that he be chosen by the like suffrage, and set apart by prayer, and the like imposition of hands.[3]

[1] **Acts 14:23** (**Geneva Bible**) And when they had ordained them Elders by election in every Church, and prayed, and fasted, they commended them to the Lord in whom they believed. [Editor's note: The Confession points to the 'original'. Stephen's Textus Receptus (1550) reads χειροτονησαντες δε αυτοις πρεσβυτερους κατ εκκλησιαν προσευξαμενοι μετα νηστειων παρεθεντο αυτους τω κυριω εις ον πεπιστευκεισαν.]

[2] **1 Tim. 4:14** Neglect not the gift that is in thee, which was given thee by prophecy, with the laying on of the hands of the presbytery.

[3] **Acts 6:3** Wherefore, brethren, look ye out among you seven men of honest report, full of the Holy Ghost and wisdom, whom we may appoint over this business. **5** And the saying pleased the whole multitude: and they chose Stephen, a man full of faith and of the Holy Ghost, and Philip, and Prochorus, and Nicanor, and Timon, and Parmenas, and Nicolas a proselyte of Antioch: **6** Whom they set before the apostles: and when they had prayed, they laid their hands on them.

10. The work of pastors being constantly to attend the service of *Christ*, in his churches, in the ministry of the word, and prayer, with watching for their souls, as they that must give an account to him;[1] it is incumbent on the churches to whom they minister, not only to give them all due respect, but also to communicate to them of all their good things according to their ability,[2] so as they may have a comfortable supply, without being themselves entangled in secular affairs;[3] and may also be capable of exercising hospitality toward others;[4] and this is required by the law of nature, and by the express order of our Lord Jesus, who hath ordained that they that preach the gospel, should live of the gospel.[5]

[1] **Acts 6:4** But we will give ourselves continually to prayer, and to the ministry of the word. **Heb. 13:17** Obey them that have the rule over you, and submit yourselves: for they watch for your souls, as they that must give account, that they may do it with joy, and not with grief: for that is unprofitable for you.

[2] **1 Tim. 5:17** Let the elders that rule well be counted worthy of double honour, especially they who labour in the word and doctrine. **18** For the scripture saith, Thou shalt not muzzle the ox that treadeth out the corn. And, The labourer is worthy of his reward. **Gal. 6:6** Let him that is taught in the word communicate unto him that teacheth in all good things. **7** Be not deceived; God is not mocked: for whatsoever a man soweth, that shall he also reap.

[3] **2 Tim. 2:4** No man that warreth entangleth himself with the affairs of this life; that he may please him who hath chosen him to be a soldier.

[4] **1 Tim. 3:2** A bishop then must be blameless, the husband of one wife, vigilant, sober, of good behaviour, given to hospitality, apt to teach.

[5] **1 Cor. 9:6–14.**

XXVI. OF THE CHURCH

11. Although it be incumbent on the bishops or pastors of the churches to be instant in preaching the word, by way of office; yet the work of preaching the word is not so peculiarly confined to them; but that others also gifted, and fitted by the Holy *Spirit* for it, and approved, and called by the *church,* may and ought to perform it.[1]

> [1] **Acts 11:19** Now they which were scattered abroad upon the persecution that arose about Stephen travelled as far as Phenice, and Cyprus, and Antioch, preaching the word to none but unto the Jews only. 20 And some of them were men of Cyprus and Cyrene, which, when they were come to Antioch, spake unto the Grecians, preaching the Lord Jesus. 21 And the hand of the Lord was with them: and a great number believed, and turned unto the Lord. **1 Pet. 4:10** As every man hath received the gift, even so minister the same one to another, as good stewards of the manifold grace of God. 11 If any man speak, let him speak as the oracles of God; if any man minister, let him do it as of the ability which God giveth: that God in all things may be glorified through Jesus Christ, to whom be praise and dominion for ever and ever. Amen.

12. As all believers are bound to join themselves to particular *churches,* when and where they have opportunity so to do; so all that are admitted unto the privileges of a *church,* are also under the censures and government thereof, according to the rule of *Christ.*[1]

> [1] **1 Thess. 5:14** Now we exhort you, brethren, warn them that are unruly, comfort the feebleminded, support the weak, be patient toward all men. **2 Thess. 3:6** Now we command you, brethren, in the name of our Lord Jesus Christ, that ye withdraw yourselves

from every brother that walketh disorderly, and not after the tradition which he received of us. **14** And if any man obey not our word by this epistle, note that man, and have no company with him, that he may be ashamed. **15** Yet count him not as an enemy, but admonish him as a brother.

13. No church members upon any offence taken by them, having performed their duty required of them towards the person they are offended at, ought to disturb any *church* order, or absent themselves from the assemblies of the *church,* or administration of any ordinances, upon the account of such offence at any of their fellow members; but to wait upon *Christ,* in the further proceeding of the *church*.[1]

[1] **Matt. 18:15** Moreover if thy brother shall trespass against thee, go and tell him his fault between thee and him alone: if he shall hear thee, thou hast gained thy brother. **16** But if he will not hear thee, then take with thee one or two more, that in the mouth of two or three witnesses every word may be established. **17** And if he shall neglect to hear them, tell it unto the church: but if he neglect to hear the church, let him be unto thee as an heathen man and a publican. **Eph. 4:2** With all lowliness and meekness, with longsuffering, forbearing one another in love; **3** Endeavouring to keep the unity of the Spirit in the bond of peace.

14. As each *church,* and all the members of it are bound to pray continually, for the good and prosperity of all the *churches* of *Christ,* in all places;[1] and upon all occasions to further it (every one within the bounds of their places, and callings, in the exercise of their gifts and graces) so the

XXVI. OF THE CHURCH

churches (when planted by the providence of God so as they may enjoy opportunity and advantage for it) ought to hold communion amongst themselves for their peace, increase of love, and mutual edification.[2]

> [1] **Eph. 6:18** Praying always with all prayer and supplication in the Spirit, and watching thereunto with all perseverance and supplication for all saints. **Ps. 122:6** Pray for the peace of Jerusalem: they shall prosper that love thee.
>
> [2] **Rom. 16:1** I commend unto you Phebe our sister, which is a servant of the church which is at Cenchrea: **2** That ye receive her in the Lord, as becometh saints, and that ye assist her in whatsoever business she hath need of you: for she hath been a succourer of many, and of myself also. **3 John 8** We therefore ought to receive such, that we might be fellowhelpers to the truth. **9** I wrote unto the church: but Diotrephes, who loveth to have the preeminence among them, receiveth us not. **10** Wherefore, if I come, I will remember his deeds which he doeth, prating against us with malicious words: and not content therewith, neither doth he himself receive the brethren, and forbiddeth them that would, and casteth them out of the church.

15. In cases of difficulties or differences, either in point of doctrine, or administration; wherein either the churches in general are concerned, or any one church in their peace, union, and edification; or any member, or members, of any church are injured, in or by any proceedings in censures not agreeable to truth, and order: it is according to the mind of Christ, that many churches holding communion together, do by their messengers meet to consider, and give their advice, in or about that matter in difference, to be reported to all the

churches concerned;[1] howbeit these messengers assembled are not entrusted with any church-power properly so called; or with any jurisdiction over the Churches themselves, to exercise any censures either over any churches, or persons: or to impose their determination on the churches, or officers.[2]

[1] **Acts 15:2** When therefore Paul and Barnabas had no small dissension and disputation with them, they determined that Paul and Barnabas, and certain other of them, should go up to Jerusalem unto the apostles and elders about this question. 4 And when they were come to Jerusalem, they were received of the church, and of the apostles and elders, and they declared all things that God had done with them. 6 And the apostles and elders came together for to consider of this matter. 22 Then pleased it the apostles and elders with the whole church, to send chosen men of their own company to Antioch with Paul and Barnabas; namely, Judas surnamed Barsabas and Silas, chief men among the brethren: 23 And they wrote letters by them after this manner; The apostles and elders and brethren send greeting unto the brethren which are of the Gentiles in Antioch and Syria and Cilicia. 25 It seemed good unto us, being assembled with one accord, to send chosen men unto you with our beloved Barnabas and Paul.

[2] **2 Cor. 1:24** Not for that we have dominion over your faith, but are helpers of your joy: for by faith ye stand. **1 John 4:1** Beloved, believe not every spirit, but try the spirits whether they are of God: because many false prophets are gone out into the world.

27

OF THE COMMUNION OF SAINTS

ALL *SAINTS* THAT are united to Jesus Christ their *head*, by his Spirit, and faith; although they are not made thereby one person with him, have fellowship in his graces, sufferings, death, resurrection, and glory;[1] and being united to one another in love, they have communion in each other's gifts, and graces;[2] and are obliged to the performance of such duties, public and private, in an orderly way, as do conduce to their mutual good, both in the inward and outward man.[3]

[1] **1 John 1:3** That which we have seen and heard declare we unto you, that ye also may have fellowship with us: and truly our fellowship is with the Father, and with his Son Jesus Christ. **John 1:16** And of his fulness have all we received, and grace for grace. **Phil. 3:10** That I may know him, and the power of his resurrection, and the fellowship of his sufferings, being made conformable unto his death. **Rom. 6:5** For if we have been planted together in the likeness of his death, we shall be also in the likeness of his resurrection: **6** Knowing this, that our old man is crucified with him, that the body of sin might be destroyed, that henceforth we should not serve sin.

[2] **Eph. 4:15** But speaking the truth in love, may grow up into him in all things, which is the head, even Christ: **16** From whom the whole body fitly joined together and compacted by that which every joint supplieth, according to the effectual working in the measure of every part, maketh increase of the body unto the edifying of itself in love. **1 Cor. 12:7** But the manifestation of the Spirit is given to every man to profit withal. **1 Cor. 3:21** Therefore let no man glory in men. For all things are yours; **22** Whether Paul, or Apollos, or Cephas, or the world, or life, or death, or things present, or things to come; all are yours; **23** And ye are Christ's; and Christ is God's.

[3] **1 Thess. 5:11** Wherefore comfort yourselves together, and edify one another, even as also ye do. **14** Now we exhort you, brethren, warn them that are unruly, comfort the feebleminded, support the weak, be patient toward all men. **Rom. 1:12** That is, that I may be comforted together with you by the mutual faith both of you and me. **1 John 3:17** But whoso hath this world's good, and seeth his brother have need, and shutteth up his bowels of compassion from him, how dwelleth the love of God in him? **18** My little children, let us not love in word, neither in tongue; but in deed and in truth. **Gal. 6:10** As we have therefore opportunity, let us do good unto all men, especially unto them who are of the household of faith.

2. *Saints* by profession are bound to maintain an holy fellowship and communion in the worship of God, and in performing such other spiritual services, as tend to their mutual edification;[1] as also in relieving each other in outward things according to their several abilities, and necessities;[2] which communion according to the rule of the gospel, though especially to be exercised by them, in the relations wherein they stand, whether in families,[3] or churches;[4] yet as God offereth

XXVII. OF THE COMMUNION OF SAINTS

opportunity is to be extended to all the household of faith, even all those who in every place call upon the name of the Lord Jesus; nevertheless their communion one with another as *saints,* doth not take away or infringe, the title or propriety, which each man hath in his goods and possessions.[5]

[1] **Heb. 10:24** And let us consider one another to provoke unto love and to good works: **25** Not forsaking the assembling of ourselves together, as the manner of some is; but exhorting one another: and so much the more, as ye see the day approaching. **With Heb. 3:12** Take heed, brethren, lest there be in any of you an evil heart of unbelief, in departing from the living God. **13** But exhort one another daily, while it is called To day; lest any of you be hardened through the deceitfulness of sin.

[2] ***Acts 11:29** Then the disciples, every man according to his ability, determined to send relief unto the brethren which dwelt in Judaea: **30** Which also they did, and sent it to the elders by the hands of Barnabas and Saul.

[3] **Eph. 6:4** And, ye fathers, provoke not your children to wrath: but bring them up in the nurture and admonition of the Lord.

[4] **1 Cor. 12:14–27.**

[5] **Acts 5:4** Whiles it remained, was it not thine own? and after it was sold, was it not in thine own power? why hast thou conceived this thing in thine heart? thou hast not lied unto men, but unto God. **Eph. 4:28** Let him that stole steal no more: but rather let him labour, working with his hands the thing which is good, that he may have to give to him that needeth.

28

OF BAPTISM AND THE LORD'S SUPPER

BAPTISM AND THE Lord's supper are ordinances of positive, and sovereign institution; appointed by the Lord Jesus the only law-giver, to be continued in his Church to the end of the world.[1]

> [1] **Matt. 28:19** Go ye therefore, and teach all nations, baptizing them in the name of the Father, and of the Son, and of the Holy Ghost: **20** Teaching them to observe all things whatsoever I have commanded you: and, lo, I am with you alway, even unto the end of the world. Amen. **1 Cor. 11:26** For as often as ye eat this bread, and drink this cup, ye do shew the Lord's death till he come.

2. These holy appointments are to be administered by those only, who are qualified and thereunto called according to the commission of Christ.[1]

> [1] **Matt. 28:19** Go ye therefore, and teach all nations, baptizing them in the name of the Father, and of the Son, and of the Holy

Ghost. **1 Cor. 4:1** Let a man so account of us, as of the ministers of Christ, and stewards of the mysteries of God.

29

OF BAPTISM

BAPTISM IS AN ordinance of the New Testament, ordained by Jesus Christ, to be unto the party baptized, a sign of his fellowship with him, in his death, and resurrection; of his being engrafted into him;[1] of remission of sins;[2] and of his giving up unto God through Jesus Christ to live and walk in newness of life.[3]

[1] **Rom. 6:3** Know ye not, that so many of us as were baptized into Jesus Christ were baptized into his death? 4 Therefore we are buried with him by baptism into death: that like as Christ was raised up from the dead by the glory of the Father, even so we also should walk in newness of life. 5 For if we have been planted together in the likeness of his death, we shall be also in the likeness of his resurrection. **Col. 2:12** Buried with him in baptism, wherein also ye are risen with him through the faith of the operation of God, who hath raised him from the dead. **Gal. 3:27** For as many of you as have been baptized into Christ have put on Christ.

[2] **Mark 1:4** John did baptize in the wilderness, and preach the baptism of repentance for the remission of sins. *__Acts 22:16__ And

now why tarriest thou? arise, and be baptized, and wash away thy sins, calling on the name of the Lord.

³ **Rom. 6:2** God forbid. How shall we, that are dead to sin, live any longer therein? 4 Therefore we are buried with him by baptism into death: that like as Christ was raised up from the dead by the glory of the Father, even so we also should walk in newness of life.

2. Those who do actually profess repentance towards *God*, faith in, and obedience, to our Lord Jesus, are the only proper subjects of this ordinance.[1]

¹ **Mark 16:16** He that believeth and is baptized shall be saved; but he that believeth not shall be damned. **Acts 8:36** And as they went on their way, they came unto a certain water: and the eunuch said, See, here is water; what doth hinder me to be baptized? 37 And Philip said, If thou believest with all thine heart, thou mayest. And he answered and said, I believe that Jesus Christ is the Son of God.

3. The outward element to be used in this ordinance is water, wherein the party is to be baptized, in the name of the Father, and of the Son, and of the Holy Spirit.[1]

¹ **Matt. 28:19** Go ye therefore, and teach all nations, baptizing them in the name of the Father, and of the Son, and of the Holy Ghost: 20 Teaching them to observe all things whatsoever I have commanded you: and, lo, I am with you alway, even unto the end of the world. Amen. **With Acts 8:38** And he commanded the chariot to stand still: and they went down both into the water, both Philip and the eunuch; and he baptized him.

XXIX. OF BAPTISM

4. Immersion, or dipping of the person in water, is necessary to the due administration of this ordinance.[1]

[1] **Matt. 3:16** And Jesus, when he was baptized, went up straightway out of the water: and, lo, the heavens were opened unto him, and he saw the Spirit of God descending like a dove, and lighting upon him. **John 3:23** And John also was baptizing in Aenon near to Salim, because there was much water there: and they came, and were baptized.

30

OF THE LORD'S SUPPER

THE SUPPER OF the Lord Jesus was instituted by him, the same night wherein he was betrayed, to be observed in his churches unto the end of the world, for the perpetual remembrance, and showing forth the sacrifice of himself in his death, confirmation of the faith of believers in all the benefits thereof, their spiritual nourishment, and growth in him, their further engagement in, and to, all duties which they owe unto him;[1] and to be a bond and pledge of their communion with him, and with each other.[2]

---

[1] **1 Cor. 11:23** For I have received of the Lord that which also I delivered unto you, That the Lord Jesus the same night in which he was betrayed took bread: **24** And when he had given thanks, he brake it, and said, Take, eat: this is my body, which is broken for you: this do in remembrance of me. **25** After the same manner also he took the cup, when he had supped, saying, This cup is the new testament in my blood: this do ye, as oft as ye drink it, in remembrance of me. **26** For as often as ye eat this bread, and drink this cup, ye do shew the Lord's death till he come.

[2] **1 Cor. 10:16** The cup of blessing which we bless, is it not the communion of the blood of Christ? The bread which we break, is it not the communion of the body of Christ? **17** For we being many are one bread, and one body: for we are all partakers of that one bread. **21** Ye cannot drink the cup of the Lord, and the cup of devils: ye cannot be partakers of the Lord's table, and of the table of devils.

2. In this ordinance Christ is not offered up to his Father, nor any real sacrifice made at all, for remission of sin of the quick or dead; but only a memorial of that one offering up of himself, by himself, upon the cross, once for all;[1] and a spiritual oblation of all possible praise unto God for the same;[2] so that the Popish sacrifice of the Mass (as they call it) is most abominable, injurious to Christ's own only sacrifice, the alone propitiation for all the sins of the elect.

[1] **Heb. 9:25** Nor yet that he should offer himself often, as the high priest entereth into the holy place every year with blood of others; **26** For then must he often have suffered since the foundation of the world: but now once in the end of the world hath he appeared to put away sin by the sacrifice of himself. **28** So Christ was once offered to bear the sins of many; and unto them that look for him shall he appear the second time without sin unto salvation.

[2] **1 Cor. 11:24** And when he had given thanks, he brake it, and said, Take, eat: this is my body, which is broken for you: this do in remembrance of me. **Matt. 26:26** And as they were eating, Jesus took bread, and blessed it, and brake it, and gave it to the disciples, and said, Take, eat; this is my body. **27** And he took the cup, and gave thanks, and gave it to them, saying, Drink ye all of it.

3. The Lord Jesus hath in this ordinance appointed his ministers to pray, and bless the elements of bread and wine, and thereby to set them apart from a common to an holy use, and to take and break the bread; to take the cup, and (they communicating also themselves) to give both to the communicants.[1]

[1] ***1 Cor. 11:23** For I have received of the Lord that which also I delivered unto you, That the Lord Jesus the same night in which he was betrayed took bread: **24** And when he had given thanks, he brake it, and said, Take, eat: this is my body, which is broken for you: this do in remembrance of me. **25** After the same manner also he took the cup, when he had supped, saying, This cup is the new testament in my blood: this do ye, as oft as ye drink it, in remembrance of me. **26** For as often as ye eat this bread, and drink this cup, ye do shew the Lord's death till he come.

4. The denial of the cup to the people, worshipping the elements, the lifting them up, or carrying them about for adoration, and reserving them for any pretended religious use, are all contrary to the nature of this ordinance, and to the institution of Christ.[1]

[1] **Matt. 26:26** And as they were eating, Jesus took bread, and blessed it, and brake it, and gave it to the disciples, and said, Take, eat; this is my body. **27** And he took the cup, and gave thanks, and gave it to them, saying, Drink ye all of it; **28** For this is my blood of the new testament, which is shed for many for the remission of sins. **Matt. 15:9** But in vain they do worship me, teaching for doctrines the commandments of men. **Exod. 20:4** Thou shalt not make unto thee any graven image, or any

likeness of any thing that is in heaven above, or that is in the earth beneath, or that is in the water under the earth. 5 Thou shalt not bow down thyself to them, nor serve them: for I the LORD thy God am a jealous God, visiting the iniquity of the fathers upon the children unto the third and fourth generation of them that hate me.

5. The outward elements in this ordinance, duly set apart to the uses ordained by Christ, have such relation to him crucified, as that truly, although in terms used figuratively, they are sometimes called by the name of the things they represent, to wit, the body and blood of Christ;[1] albeit in substance, and nature, they still remain truly, and only bread, and wine, as they were before.[2]

[1] **1 Cor. 11:27** Wherefore whosoever shall eat this bread, and drink this cup of the Lord, unworthily, shall be guilty of the body and blood of the Lord.

[2] **1 Cor. 11:26** For as often as ye eat this bread, and drink this cup, ye do shew the Lord's death till he come. **28** But let a man examine himself, and so let him eat of that bread, and drink of that cup.

6. That doctrine which maintains a change of the substance of bread and wine, into the substance of Christ's body and blood (commonly called transubstantiation) by consecration of a priest, or by any other way, is repugnant not to Scripture alone,[1] but even to common sense and reason; overthroweth the nature of the ordinance, and hath been and is the cause of manifold superstitions, yea, of gross idolatries.[2]

[1] **Acts 3:21** Whom the heaven must receive until the times of restitution of all things, which God hath spoken by the mouth of all his holy prophets since the world began. **Luke 24:6** He is not here, but is risen: remember how he spake unto you when he was yet in Galilee. 39 Behold my hands and my feet, that it is I myself: handle me, and see; for a spirit hath not flesh and bones, as ye see me have.

[2] **1 Cor. 11:24** And when he had given thanks, he brake it, and said, Take, eat: this is my body, which is broken for you: this do in remembrance of me. 25 After the same manner also he took the cup, when he had supped, saying, This cup is the new testament in my blood: this do ye, as oft as ye drink it, in remembrance of me.

7. Worthy receivers, outwardly partaking of the visible elements in this ordinance, do then also inwardly by faith, really and indeed, yet not carnally, and corporally, but spiritually receive, and feed upon Christ crucified and all the benefits of his death: the body and blood of *Christ,* being then not corporally, or carnally, but spiritually present to the faith of believers, in that ordinance, as the elements themselves are to their outward senses.[1]

[1] **1 Cor. 10:16** The cup of blessing which we bless, is it not the communion of the blood of Christ? The bread which we break, is it not the communion of the body of Christ? **1 Cor. 11:23** For I have received of the Lord that which also I delivered unto you, That the Lord Jesus the same night in which he was betrayed took bread: 24 And when he had given thanks, he brake it, and said, Take, eat: this is my body, which is broken for you: this do in remembrance of me. 25 After the same manner also he took the cup, when he had supped, saying, This cup is the new testament

in my blood: this do ye, as oft as ye drink it, in remembrance of me. **26** For as often as ye eat this bread, and drink this cup, ye do shew the Lord's death till he come.

8. All ignorant and ungodly persons, as they are unfit to enjoy communion with *Christ;*[1] so are they unworthy of the Lord's table; and cannot without great sin against him, while they remain such, partake of these holy mysteries, or be admitted thereunto: yea whosoever shall receive unworthily are guilty of the body and blood of the Lord, eating and drinking judgement to themselves.[2]

---

[1] **2 Cor. 6:14** Be ye not unequally yoked together with unbelievers: for what fellowship hath righteousness with unrighteousness? and what communion hath light with darkness? **15** And what concord hath Christ with Belial? or what part hath he that believeth with an infidel?

[2] **1 Cor. 11:29** For he that eateth and drinketh unworthily, eateth and drinketh damnation to himself, not discerning the Lord's body. **Matt. 7:6** Give not that which is holy unto the dogs, neither cast ye your pearls before swine, lest they trample them under their feet, and turn again and rend you.

31

OF THE STATE OF MAN AFTER DEATH AND OF THE RESURRECTION OF THE DEAD

THE BODIES OF men after death return to dust, and see corruption;[1] but their souls (which neither die nor sleep) having an immortal subsistence, immediately return to God who gave them:[2] the souls of the righteous being then made perfect in holiness, are received into paradise where they are with *Christ,* and behold the face of *God,* in light and glory; waiting for the full redemption of their bodies;[3] and the souls of the wicked are cast into hell; where they remain in torment and utter darkness, reserved to the judgement of the great day;[4] besides these two places for souls separated from their bodies, the Scripture acknowledgeth none.

[1] **Gen. 3:19** In the sweat of thy face shalt thou eat bread, till thou return unto the ground; for out of it wast thou taken: for dust thou art, and unto dust shalt thou return. **Acts 13:36** For David, after he had served his own generation by the will of God, fell on sleep, and was laid unto his fathers, and saw corruption.

[2] **Eccl. 12:7** Then shall the dust return to the earth as it was: and the spirit shall return unto God who gave it.

[3] **Luke 23:43** And Jesus said unto him, Verily I say unto thee, To day shalt thou be with me in paradise. **2 Cor. 5:1** For we know that if our earthly house of this tabernacle were dissolved, we have a building of God, an house not made with hands, eternal in the heavens. 6 Therefore we are always confident, knowing that, whilst we are at home in the body, we are absent from the Lord. 8 We are confident, I say, and willing rather to be absent from the body, and to be present with the Lord. **Phil. 1:23** For I am in a strait betwixt two, having a desire to depart, and to be with Christ; which is far better. **Heb. 12:23** To the general assembly and church of the firstborn, which are written in heaven, and to God the Judge of all, and to the spirits of just men made perfect.

[4] **Jude 6** And the angels which kept not their first estate, but left their own habitation, he hath reserved in everlasting chains under darkness unto the judgment of the great day. 7 Even as Sodom and Gomorrha, and the cities about them in like manner, giving themselves over to fornication, and going after strange flesh, are set forth for an example, suffering the vengeance of eternal fire. **1 Pet. 3:19** By which also he went and preached unto the spirits in prison. **Luke 16:23** And in hell he lift up his eyes, being in torments, and seeth Abraham afar off, and Lazarus in his bosom. 24 And he cried and said, Father Abraham, have mercy on me, and send Lazarus, that he may dip the tip of his finger in water, and cool my tongue; for I am tormented in this flame.

2. At the last day such of the saints as are found alive shall not sleep but be changed;[1] and all the dead shall be raised up with the self same bodies, and none other;[2] although with different qualities, which shall be united again to their souls for ever.[3]

XXXI. OF THE STATE OF MAN AFTER DEATH

[1] **1 Cor. 15:51** Behold, I shew you a mystery; We shall not all sleep, but we shall all be changed, **52** In a moment, in the twinkling of an eye, at the last trump: for the trumpet shall sound, and the dead shall be raised incorruptible, and we shall be changed. **1 Thess. 4:17** Then we which are alive and remain shall be caught up together with them in the clouds, to meet the Lord in the air: and so shall we ever be with the Lord.

[2] **Job 19:26** And though after my skin worms destroy this body, yet in my flesh shall I see God: **27** Whom I shall see for myself, and mine eyes shall behold, and not another; though my reins be consumed within me.

[3] **1 Cor. 15:42** So also is the resurrection of the dead. It is sown in corruption; it is raised in incorruption: **43** It is sown in dishonour; it is raised in glory: it is sown in weakness; it is raised in power.

3. The bodies of the unjust shall by the power of *Christ* be raised to dishonour; the bodies of the just by his spirit unto honour, and be made conformable to his own glorious body.[1]

[1] **Acts 24:15** And have hope toward God, which they themselves also allow, that there shall be a resurrection of the dead, both of the just and unjust. **John 5:28** Marvel not at this: for the hour is coming, in the which all that are in the graves shall hear his voice, **29** And shall come forth; they that have done good, unto the resurrection of life; and they that have done evil, unto the resurrection of damnation. **Phil. 3:21** Who shall change our vile body, that it may be fashioned like unto his glorious body, according to the working whereby he is able even to subdue all things unto himself.

32

OF THE LAST JUDGEMENT

GOD HATH APPOINTED a day wherein he will judge the world in righteousness, by Jesus Christ;[1] to whom all power and judgement is given of the Father; in which day not only the apostate angels shall be judged;[2] but likewise all persons that have lived upon the Earth, shall appear before the tribunal of *Christ;* to give an account of their thoughts, words, and deeds, and to receive according to what they have done in the body, whether good or evil.[3]

[1] **Acts 17:31** Because he hath appointed a day, in the which he will judge the world in righteousness by that man whom he hath ordained; whereof he hath given assurance unto all men, in that he hath raised him from the dead. **John 5:22** For the Father judgeth no man, but hath committed all judgment unto the Son. 27 And hath given him authority to execute judgment also, because he is the Son of man.

[2] **1 Cor. 6:3** Know ye not that we shall judge angels? how much more things that pertain to this life? **Jude 6** And the angels which kept not their first estate, but left their own habitation,

he hath reserved in everlasting chains under darkness unto the judgment of the great day.

³ **2 Cor. 5:10** For we must all appear before the judgment seat of Christ; that every one may receive the things done in his body, according to that he hath done, whether it be good or bad. **Eccl. 12:14** For God shall bring every work into judgment, with every secret thing, whether it be good, or whether it be evil. **Matt. 12:36** But I say unto you, That every idle word that men shall speak, they shall give account thereof in the day of judgment. **Rom. 14:10** But why dost thou judge thy brother? or why dost thou set at nought thy brother? for we shall all stand before the judgment seat of Christ. **12** So then every one of us shall give account of himself to God. *****Matt. 25:32** And before him shall be gathered all nations: and he shall separate them one from another, as a shepherd divideth his sheep from the goats.

2. The end of God's appointing this day is for the manifestation of the glory of his mercy, in the eternal salvation of the elect; and of his justice in the eternal damnation of the reprobate, who are wicked and disobedient;[1] for then shall the righteous go into everlasting life, and receive that fullness of joy, and glory with everlasting reward, in the presence of the Lord:[2] but the wicked who know not God, and obey not the gospel of Jesus Christ, shall be cast into eternal torments, and punished with everlasting destruction, from the presence of the Lord, and from the glory of his power.[3]

[1] **Rom. 9:22** What if God, willing to shew his wrath, and to make his power known, endured with much longsuffering the vessels of wrath fitted to destruction: **23** And that he might make known the

XXXII. OF THE LAST JUDGEMENT

riches of his glory on the vessels of mercy, which he had afore prepared unto glory.

[2] **Matt. 25:21** His lord said unto him, Well done, thou good and faithful servant: thou hast been faithful over a few things, I will make thee ruler over many things: enter thou into the joy of thy lord. 34 Then shall the King say unto them on his right hand, Come, ye blessed of my Father, inherit the kingdom prepared for you from the foundation of the world. **2 Tim. 4:8** Henceforth there is laid up for me a crown of righteousness, which the Lord, the righteous judge, shall give me at that day: and not to me only, but unto all them also that love his appearing.

[3] **Matt. 25:46** And these shall go away into everlasting punishment: but the righteous into life eternal. **Mark 9:48** Where their worm dieth not, and the fire is not quenched. **2 Thess. 1:7** And to you who are troubled rest with us, when the Lord Jesus shall be revealed from heaven with his mighty angels, 8 In flaming fire taking vengeance on them that know not God, and that obey not the gospel of our Lord Jesus Christ: 9 Who shall be punished with everlasting destruction from the presence of the Lord, and from the glory of his power; 10 When he shall come to be glorified in his saints, and to be admired in all them that believe (because our testimony among you was believed) in that day.

3. As Christ would have us to be certainly persuaded that there shall be a day of judgement, both to deter all men from sin,[1] and for the greater consolation of the godly, in their adversity;[2] so will he have that day unknown to men, that they may shake off all carnal security, and be always watchful, because they know not at what hour the Lord will come;[3] and may ever be prepared to say, *Come Lord Jesus, come quickly, Amen.*[4]

[1] **2 Cor. 5:10** For we must all appear before the judgment seat of Christ; that every one may receive the things done in his body, according to that he hath done, whether it be good or bad. **11** Knowing therefore the terror of the Lord, we persuade men; but we are made manifest unto God; and I trust also are made manifest in your consciences.

[2] **2 Thess. 1:5** Which is a manifest token of the righteous judgment of God, that ye may be counted worthy of the kingdom of God, for which ye also suffer: **6** Seeing it is a righteous thing with God to recompense tribulation to them that trouble you; **7** And to you who are troubled rest with us, when the Lord Jesus shall be revealed from heaven with his mighty angels.

[3] **Mark 13:35** Watch ye therefore: for ye know not when the master of the house cometh, at even, or at midnight, or at the cockcrowing, or in the morning: **36** Lest coming suddenly he find you sleeping. **37** And what I say unto you I say unto all, Watch. ***Luke 12:35** Let your loins be girded about, and your lights burning; **36** And ye yourselves like unto men that wait for their lord, when he will return from the wedding; that when he cometh and knocketh, they may open unto him immediately.

[4] **Rev. 22:20** He which testifieth these things saith, Surely I come quickly. Amen. Even so, come, Lord Jesus.

AN APPENDIX

WHOSOEVER READS, AND impartially considers what we have in our forgoing confession declared, may readily perceive, that we do not only concenter with all other true Christians on the word of God (revealed in the Scriptures of truth) as the foundation and rule of our faith and worship. But that we have also industriously endeavoured to manifest, that in the fundamental articles of Christianity we mind the same things, and have therefore expressed our belief in the same words, that have on the like occasion been spoken by other societies of Christians before us.

This we have done, that those who are desirous to know the principles of religion which we hold and practice, may take an estimate from our selves (who jointly concur in this work) and may not be misguided, either by undue reports; or by the ignorance or errors of particular persons, who going under the same name with our selves, may give an occasion of scandalizing the truth we profess.

And although we do differ from our brethren who are paedobaptists; in the subject and administration of baptism, and such other circumstances as have a necessary dependence on our observance of that ordinance, and do frequent our own assemblies for our mutual edification, and discharge of those duties, and services which we owe unto God, and in his fear to each other: yet we would not be from hence misconstrued, as if the discharge of our own consciences herein, did any ways disoblige or alienate our affections, or conversation from any others that fear the Lord; but that we may and do as we have opportunity participate of the labours of those, whom God hath endued with abilities above our selves, and qualified, and called to the ministry of the *word,* earnestly desiring to approve our selves to be such, as follow after peace with holiness, and therefore we always keep that blessed *irenicum,* or healing *word* of the Apostle before our eyes; 'if in any thing ye be otherwise minded, God shall reveal even this unto you; nevertheless whereto we have already attained; let us walk by the same rule, let us mind the same thing' (Phil. 3:15–16).

Let it not therefore be judged of us (because much hath been written on this subject, and yet we continue this our practice different from others) that it is out of obstinacy, but rather as the truth is, that we do herein according to the best of our understandings worship God, out of a pure mind yielding obedience to his precept, in that method which we take to be most agreeable to the Scriptures of truth, and primitive practice.

It would not become us to give any such intimation, as should carry a semblance that what we do in the service of God is with a doubting conscience, or with any such temper of mind that we do thus for the present, with a reservation that we will do otherwise hereafter upon more mature deliberation; nor have we any cause so to do, being fully persuaded, that what we do is agreeable to the will of God. Yet we do heartily propose this, that if any of the servants of our Lord Jesus shall, in the Spirit of meekness, attempt to convince us of any mistake either in judgement or practice, we shall diligently ponder his arguments; and accompt him our chiefest friend that shall be an instrument to convert us from any error that is in our ways, for we cannot wittingly do any thing against the truth, but all things for the truth.

And therefore we have endeavoured seriously to consider, what hath been already offered for our satisfaction in this point; and are loath to say any more lest we should be esteemed desirous of renewed contests thereabout: yet forasmuch as it may justly be expected that we show some reason, why we cannot acquiesce in what hath been urged against us; we shall with as much brevity as may consist with plainness, endeavour to satisfy the expectation of those that shall peruse what we now publish in this matter also.

1. As to those Christians who consent with us, *that repentance from dead works, and faith towards God, and our Lord Jesus Christ, is required in persons to be baptized;* and do therefore supply the defect of the (infant being uncapable of making confession of either) by others who do undertake these things for it. Although we do find by Church history that this hath been a very ancient practice; yet considering, that the same Scripture which does caution us against censuring our brother, with whom we shall all stand before the judgement seat of Christ, does also instruct us, *that every one of us shall give an accompt of himself to God, and whatsoever is not of faith is sin* (Rom. 14:4, 10, 12, 23). Therefore we cannot for our own parts be persuaded in our own minds, to build such a practice as this, upon an unwritten tradition: but do rather choose in all points of faith and worship, to have recourse to the holy Scriptures, for the information of our judgement, and regulation of our practice; being well assured that a conscientious attending thereto, is the best way to prevent, and rectify our defects and errors (2 Tim. 3:16–17). And if any such case happen to be debated between Christians, which is not plainly determinable by the Scriptures, we think it safest to leave such things undecided until the second coming of our Lord Jesus; as they did in the Church of old, until there should arise a priest with *Urim* and *Thummim,* that might certainly inform them of the mind of God thereabout (Ezra 2:62–63).

2. As for those our Christian brethren who do ground their arguments for infants baptism, upon a presumed federal holiness, or church-membership, we conceive they are deficient in this, that albeit this covenant-holiness and membership should be as is supposed, in reference unto the infants of believers; yet no command

for infant baptism does immediately and directly result from such a quality, or relation.

All instituted worship receives its sanction from the precept, and is to be thereby governed in all the necessary circumstances thereof.

So it was in the covenant that God made with *Abraham* and his seed. The sign whereof was appropriated only to the male, notwithstanding that the female seed as well as the male were comprehended in the covenant and part of the Church of God; neither was this sign to be affixed to any male infant till he was eight days old, albeit he was within the covenant from the first moment of his life; nor could the danger of death, or any other supposed necessity, warrant the circumcising of him before the set time, nor was there any cause for it; the commination of being cut off from his people, being only upon the neglect, or contempt of the precept.

Righteous *Lot* was nearly related to *Abraham* in the flesh, and contemporary with him, when this covenant was made; yet inasmuch as he did not descend from his loins, nor was of his household family (although he was of the same household of faith with *Abraham*) yet neither *Lot* himself nor any of his posterity (because of their descent from him) were signed with the signature of this covenant that was made with *Abraham* and his seed.

This may suffice to show, that where there was both an express covenant, and a sign thereof (such a covenant as did separate the persons with whom it was made, and all their offspring from all the rest of the world, as a people holy unto the Lord, and did constitute them the visible Church of God, though not comprehensive of all the faithful in the world), yet the sign of this covenant was not affixed to all the persons that were within this covenant, nor to any of them till the prefixed season; nor to other faithful servants of God, that were not of descent from *Abraham*. And consequently that it depends purely upon the will of the Law-giver, to determine what shall be the sign of his covenant, unto whom, at what season, and upon what terms, it shall be affixed.

If our brethren do suppose baptism to be the seal of the covenant which God makes with every believer (of which the Scriptures are altogether silent) it is not our concern to contend with them herein; yet we conceive the seal of that covenant is the indwelling of the Spirit of Christ in the particular and individual persons in whom he resides, and nothing else, neither do they or we suppose that baptism is in any such manner substituted in the place of circumcision, as to have the same (and no other) latitude, extent, or terms, than circumcision had; for that was suited only for the male children, baptism is an ordinance suited for every believer, whether male, or female. That extended to all the males that were born in *Abraham's* house, or bought with his money, equally with the males that proceeded from his own loins; but baptism is not so far extended in any true Christian church that we know of, as to be administered to all the poor infidel servants, that the members thereof purchase for their service, and introduce into their families; nor to the children born of them in their house.

But we conceive the same parity of reasoning may hold for the ordinance of baptism as for that of circumcision; Exodus 12:49, *viz.* one law for the stranger, as for the home born: if any desire to be admitted to all the ordinances, and privileges of God's house, the door is open; upon the same terms that any one person was ever admitted to all, or any of those privileges, that belong to the Christian Church; may all persons of right challenge the like admission.

As for that text of Scripture, *'he received circumcision a seal of the righteousness of the faith which he had yet being uncircumcised'* (Rom. 4:11); we conceive if the Apostle's scope in that place be duly attended to, it will appear that no argument can be taken from thence to enforce infant baptism; and forasmuch as we find a full and fair account of those words given by the learned Dr *Lightfoot* (a man not to be suspected of partiality in this controversy) in his *Horae Hebraicae,* on 1 Cor. 7:19 (pp. 42–43), we shall transcribe his words at large, without any comment of our own upon them:

> Circumcision is nothing, if we respect the time, for now it was without use, that end of it being especially fulfilled; for which it had been instituted: this end the Apostle declares in these words, Rom. 4:11, 'σφραγῖδα, etc.' But I fear that by most translations they are not sufficiently suited to the end of circumcision, and the scope of the Apostle whilst something of their own is by them inserted.

And after the Doctor has represented diverse versions of the words agreeing for the most part in sense with that which we have in our Bibles he thus proceeds:

> Other versions are to the same purpose; as if circumcision was given to Abraham for a Seal of that Righteousness which he had being yet uncircumcised, which we will not deny to be in some sense true, but we believe that circumcision had chiefly a far different respect.
>
> Give me leave thus to render the words; *And he received the sign of circumcision, a seal of the Righteousness of Faith, which was to be in the uncircumcision, which was to be* (I say) not *which had been,* not that which *Abraham* had whilst he was yet uncircumcised; but that which his uncircumcised seed should have, that is the Gentiles, who in time to come should imitate the faith of *Abraham.*
>
> Now consider well on what occasion circumcision was instituted unto *Abraham,* setting before thine eyes the history thereof, Gen. 17.
>
> This promise is first made unto him, *Thou shalt be the father*

of many nations (in what sense the Apostle explaineth in that chapter) and then there is subjoined a double seal for the confirmation of the thing, to wit, the change of the name *Abram* into *Abraham,* and the institution of circumcision (v. 4). *Behold as for me, my Covenant is with thee, and thou shalt be the father of many nations.* Wherefore was his name called *Abraham?* For the sealing of this promise: *thou shalt be the father of many nations.* And wherefore was circumcision instituted to him? For the sealing of the same promise: *thou shalt be the father of many nations.* So that this is the sense of the Apostle, most agreeable to the institution of circumcision; he received the sign of circumcision, a seal of the Righteousness of Faith which in time to come the uncircumcision (or the Gentiles) should have and obtain.

Abraham had a twofold seed, *natural,* of the Jews; and *faithful,* of the believing Gentiles: his natural seed was signed with the sign of circumcision, first indeed for the distinguishing of them from all other nations whilst they as yet were not the seed of *Abraham,* but especially for the memorial of the justification of the Gentiles by faith, when at length they should become his seed. Therefore circumcision was of right to cease, when the Gentiles were brought in to the faith, forasmuch as then it had obtained its last and chief end, and thenceforth *circumcision is nothing.*

Thus far he, which we earnestly desire may be seriously weighed, for we plead not his authority, but the evidence of truth in his words.

3. Of whatsoever nature the holiness of the children mentioned be (1 Cor. 7:12), yet they who do conclude that all such children (whether infants or of riper years) have from hence an immediate right to baptism, do as we conceive put more into the conclusion, than will be found in the premisses.

For although we do not determine positively concerning the Apostle's scope in the holiness here mentioned, so as to say it is this, or that, and no other thing; yet it is evident that the Apostle does by it determine not only the lawfulness but the expedience also of a believer's cohabitation with an unbeliever, in the state of marriage.

And we do think that although the Apostle's asserting of the unbelieving yokefellow to be sanctified by the believer, should carry in it somewhat more than is in the bare marriage of two infidels, because although the marriage covenant has a divine sanction so as to make the wedlock of two unbelievers a lawful action, and their conjunction and cohabitation in that respect undefiled, yet there might be no ground to suppose from thence, that both or either of their persons are thereby sanctified; and the Apostle urges the cohabitation of a believer with an infidel in the state of wedlock from this ground that the unbelieving husband is *sanctified* by the believing wife; nevertheless here you have the influence of a believer's faith *ascending from an inferior to a superior relation;* from the wife to the husband who is her head, *before it can descend to their offspring.* And therefore we say, whatever be the nature or extent of the holiness here intended, we conceive it cannot convey to the children an immediate right to baptism; because it would then be of another nature, and of a larger extent, than the root, and original from whence it is derived, for it is clear by the Apostle's argument that holiness cannot be derived to the child from the sanctity of one parent only, if either father or mother be (in the sense intended by the Apostle) unholy or unclean, so will the child be also, therefore for the production of an holy seed it is necessary that both the parents be sanctified; and this the Apostle positively asserts in the first place to be done by the believing parent, although the other be an unbeliever; and then consequentially from thence argues, the holiness of their children. Hence it follows, that as the children have no other holiness than what they derive from both their parents; so neither can they have any right by this holiness to any spiritual privilege but such as both their parents did also partake of: and therefore if the unbelieving parent (though sanctified by the believing parent) have not thereby a right to baptism, neither can we conceive, that there is any such privilege, derived to the children by their birth-holiness.

Besides if it had been the usual practice in the Apostle's days for the father or mother that did believe, to bring all their children with them to be baptized; then the holiness of the believing *Corinthians'* children, would not at all have been in question when this epistle was written; but might have been argued from their passing under that ordinance, which represented their new birth, although they had derived no holiness from their parents, by their first birth; and would have lain as an exception against the Apostle's inference, *else were your children unclean* etc. But of the sanctification of all the children of every believer by this ordinance, or any other way than what is beforementioned, the Scripture is altogether silent.

This may also be added; that if this birth holiness do qualify all the children of every believer, for the ordinance of baptism; why not for all other ordinances? For the Lord's supper as was practiced for a long time together? For if recourse be had to what the Scriptures speak generally of this subject; it will be found, that the same qualities which do entitle any person to baptism, do so also for the participation of all the ordinances, and privileges of the house of God, that are common to all believers.

Whosoever can and does interrogate his good conscience towards God when he is baptized (as every one must do that makes it to himself a sign of salvation) is capable of doing the same thing, in every other act of worship that he performs.

4. The arguments and inferences that are usually brought for, or against infant baptism from those few instances which the Scriptures afford us of whole families being baptized; are only conjectural; and therefore cannot of themselves, be conclusive on either hand:

yet in regard most that treat on this subject for infant baptism, do (as they conceive) improve these instances to the advantage of their argument: we think it meet (in like manner as in the cases before mentioned so in this) to show the invalidity of such inferences.

Cornelius worshipped God with all his *house,* the *jailer,* and *Crispus* the chief ruler of the Synagogue, believed God with each of their *houses. The household of Stephanus* addicted themselves to the ministry of the saints: so that thus far *worshipping,* and *believing* runs parallel with *baptism.* And if *Lydia,* had been a married person when she believed, it is probable her husband would also have been named by the Apostle, as in like cases, inasmuch as he would have been not only a part, but the head of that baptized household.

Who can assign any probable reason, why the Apostle should make mention of four or five households being baptized and no more? Or why he does so often vary in the method of his salutations (Rom. 16), sometimes mentioning only particular persons of great note, other times such, and the church in their house? The saints that were with them; and them belonging to *Narcissus,* who were in the Lord; thus saluting either whole families, or part of families, or only particular persons in families, considered as they were in the Lord, for if it had been an usual practice to baptize all children, with their parents; there were then many thousands of the Jews which believed, and a great number of the Gentiles, in most of the principle cities in the world, and among so many thousands, it is more than probable there would have been some thousands of households baptized; why then should the Apostle in this respect signalize one family of the Jews and three or four of the Gentiles, as particular instances in a case that was common? Whoever supposes that we do wilfully debar our children, from the benefit of any promise, or privilege, that of right belongs to the children of believing parents; they do entertain over severe thoughts of us: to be without natural affections is one of the characters of the worst of persons, in the worst of times. We do freely confess our selves guilty before the Lord, in that we have not with more circumspection and diligence trained up those that relate to us in the fear of the Lord; and do humbly and earnestly pray, that our omissions herein may be remitted, and that they may not redound to the prejudice of our selves, or any of ours: but with respect to that duty that is incumbent on us, we acknowledge our selves obliged by the precepts of God, to bring up our children in the nurture and admonition of the Lord, to teach them his fear, both by instruction and example; and should we set light by this precept, it would demonstrate that we are more vile than the unnatural heathen, that like not to retain God in their knowledge, our baptism might then be justly accompted, as no baptism to us.

There are many special promises that do encourage us as well as precepts, that do oblige us to the close pursuit of our duty herein: that God whom we serve, being jealous of his worship, threatens the visiting of the father's transgression upon the children to the third and fourth generation of them that hate him: yet does more abundantly extend his mercy, even to thousands (respecting the offspring and succeeding generations) of them that love him, and keep his commands.

When our Lord rebuked his disciples for prohibiting the access of little children that were brought to him, that he might pray over them, lay his hands upon them, and bless them, does declare, *that of such is the kingdom of God.* And the Apostle *Peter* in answer to their enquiry, that desired to know what they must do to be saved, does not only instruct them in the necessary duty of repentance and baptism; but does also thereto encourage them, by that promise which had reference both to them, and their children; if our Lord Jesus in the aforementioned place, does not respect the qualities of children (as elsewhere) as to their meekness, humility, and sincerity, and the like; but intend also that those very persons and such like, appertain to the kingdom of God, and if the Apostle *Peter* in mentioning the aforesaid promise, do respect not only the present and succeeding generations of those Jews, that heard him (in which sense the same phrase doth occur in Scripture), but also the immediate offspring of his auditors; whether the promise relate to the gift of the Holy Spirit, or of eternal life, or any grace, or privilege tending to the obtaining thereof; it is neither our concern nor our interest to confine the mercies, and promises of God, to a more narrow, or less compass than he is pleased graciously to offer and intend them; nor to have a light esteem of them; but are obliged in duty to God, and affection to our children; to plead earnestly with God and use our utmost endeavours that both our selves, and our offspring may be partakers of his mercies and gracious promises: yet we cannot from either of these texts collect a sufficient warrant for us to baptize our children before they are instructed in the principles of the Christian religion.

For as to the instance in little children, it seems by the disciples forbidding them, that they were brought upon some other account, not so frequent as baptism must be supposed to have been, if from the beginning believers' children had been admitted thereto: and no account is given whether their parents were baptized believers or not; and as to the instance of the Apostle; if the following words and practice, may be taken as an interpretation of the scope of that promise we cannot conceive it does refer to infant baptism, because the text does presently subjoin, *Then they that gladly received the word were baptized*.

That there were some believing children of believing parents in the Apostle's days is evident from the Scriptures, even such as were then in their father's family, and under their parents' tuition, and education; to whom the Apostle in several of his epistles to the churches, giveth commands to obey their parents in the Lord; and does allure their tender years to hearken to this precept, by reminding them that it is the first command with promise.

And it is recorded by him for the praise of *Timothy*, and encouragement of parents betimes to instruct, and children early to attend to godly instruction, that ἀπὸ βρέφους from a child, he had known the holy Scriptures.

The Apostle *John* rejoiced greatly when he found of the children of the elect lady walking in the truth; and the children of her elect sister join with the Apostle in his salutation.

But that this was not generally so, that all the children of believers were accounted for believers (as they would have been if they had been all baptized) may be collected from the character which the Apostle gives of persons fit to be chosen to eldership in the church which was not common to all believers; among others this is expressly one, *viz. if there be any having believing, or faithful children,* not accused of riot or unruly; and we may from the Apostle's writings on the same subject collect the reason of this qualification, *viz.* that in case the person designed for this office to teach and rule in the house of God, had children capable of it; there might be first a proof of his ability, industry, and success in this work in his own family; and private capacity, before he was ordained to the exercise of this authority in the church, in a public capacity, as a bishop in the house of God.

These things we have mentioned as having a direct reference unto the controversy between our brethren and us; other things that are more abstruse and prolix, which are frequently introduced into this controversy, but do not necessarily concern it, we have purposely avoided; that the distance between us and our brethren may not be by us made more wide; for it is our duty, and concern so far as is possible for us (retaining a good conscience towards God) to seek a more entire agreement and reconciliation with them.

We are not insensible that as to the order of God's house, and entire communion therein there are some things wherein we (as well as others) are not at a full accord among our selves, as for instance; the known principle, and state of the consciences of diverse of us, that have agreed in this Confession is such; that we cannot hold church-communion, with any other than baptized believers, and churches constituted of such; yet some others of us have a greater liberty and freedom in our spirits that way; and therefore we have purposely omitted the mention of things of that nature, that we might concur, in giving this evidence of our agreement, both among our selves, and with other good Christians, in those important articles of the Christian religion, mainly insisted on by us: and this notwithstanding we all esteem it our chief concern, both among our selves, and all others that in every place call upon the name of the Lord Jesus Christ our Lord, both theirs and ours, and love him in sincerity, to endeavour to keep the unity of the Spirit, in the bond of peace; and in order thereunto, to exercise all lowliness and meekness, with long-suffering, forbearing one another in love.

And we are persuaded if the same method were introduced into frequent practice between us and our Christian friends who agree with us in all the fundamental articles of the Christian faith (though they do not so in the subject and administration of baptism) it would soon beget a better understanding, and brotherly affection between us.

In the beginning of the Christian Church, when the doctrine of the baptism of *Christ* was not universally understood, yet those that knew only the baptism of *John,* were the disciples of the Lord Jesus; and *Apollos* an eminent minister of the gospel of Jesus.

In the beginning of the Reformation of the Christian Church, and recovery from that *Egyptian* darkness wherein our forefathers for many generations were held in bondage; upon recourse had to the Scriptures of truth, different apprehensions were conceived, which are to this time continued, concerning the practice of this ordinance.

Let not our zeal herein be misinterpreted: that God whom we serve is jealous of his worship. By his gracious providence the law thereof, is continued amongst us; and we are forewarned by what happened in the Church of the Jews, that it is necessary for every generation, and that frequently in every generation to consult the divine oracle, compare our worship with the rule, and take heed to what doctrines we receive and practice.

If the ten commands exhibited in the popish idolatrous service books had been received as the entire law of God, because they agree in number with his ten commands, and also in the substance of nine of them; the second commandment forbidding idolatry had been utterly lost.

If *Ezra* and *Nehemiah* had not made a diligent search into the particular parts of God's law, and his worship; the Feast of Tabernacles (which for many centuries of years, had not been duly observed, according to the institution, though it was retained in the general notion) would not have been kept in due order.

So may it be now as to many things relating to the service of God, which do retain the names proper to them in their first institution, but yet through inadvertency (where there is no sinister design) may vary in their circumstances, from their first institution. And if by means of any ancient defection, or of that general corruption of the service of God, and interruption of his true worship, and persecution of his servants by the anti-Christian Bishop of *Rome,* for many generations; those who do consult the word of God, cannot yet arrive at a full and mutual satisfaction among themselves, what was the practice of the primitive Christian Church, in some points relating to the *worship* of God: yet inasmuch as these things are not of the essence of Christianity, but that we agree in the fundamental doctrines thereof, we do apprehend, there is sufficient ground to lay aside all bitterness and prejudice, and in the spirit of love and meekness to embrace and own each other therein; leaving each other at liberty to perform such other services (wherein we cannot concur), apart unto God, according to the best of our understanding.